How to Draw
CELTIC
KEY PATTERNS

How to Draw
CELTIC
KEY PATTERNS

A Practical Handbook

Andy Sloss

BLANDFORD

Picts (from Latin Picti, "painted"), one of an ancient non-Celtic people who inhabited [an 'ain'] what is now eastern and northern Scotland, from Caithness to the Firth. Their name may refer to their custom of body painting or possibly tattooing. Probably descendants of pre-Celtic aborigines, the Picts were first noticed in AD 297, when a Roman writer spoke of the "Picts and Irish [Scots] attacking" Hadrian's Wall, probably with the Romans during the occupation was almost continual. Then or soon after they deemed to have developed two kingdoms, north of the Forth, a southern and a northern; but by the 7th century there was a united "Pictland," which already had been penetrated by Christianity. In 843, Kenneth I MacAlpin, king of Scots (centred in Argyll and Bute), became also king of the Picts, uniting their two lands in a new kingdom of Alba, which evolved into Scotland.

The Pictish kingdom is notable for the stylized but vigorous beauty of its carved memorial stones and crosses, the round stone towers known as brochs, or "Pictish towers," and the underground stone houses called weems or "Picts' houses," however, both predate this kingdom.

Pictish language, spoken by the Picts in northern Scotland and replaced by Gaelic after the union in the 9th century of the Pictish kingdom with the rest of Scotland. Knowledge of the Pictish language is derived from place-names, names in medieval works such as the Pictish Chronicle and the writings of Bede, inscriptions from the Pictish areas of Britain, statements about the language by medieval writers who wrote while the language was still in use, and names from northern Scotland found in classical works. Pictish was apparently a Celtic language (more closely related to Gaulish and Brythonic than to Gaelic), but some scholars think it was not Celtic, nor even Indo-European.

A Blandford Book

A Cassell Imprint
Cassell Plc, Wellington House
125 Strand, London WC2R 0BB

Distributed in the United States by Sterling Publishing Co., Inc., 387 Park Avenue South, New York, NY 10016-8810

A Cataloguing-in-Publication Data entry for this title is available from the British Library.

ISBN   0-7137-2652-0

Designed by Ben Cracknell Studios

Printed and bound in Great Britain by The Bath Press

CONTENTS

for Adèle

Coran and Jennifer

INTRODUCTION

Key patterns go way back into prehistory – there is one carved into mammoth ivory from around 15,000 BC – but the name did not exist until J. Romilly Allen coined it at the beginning of this century. He saw parallels between these patterns and the shape of the traditional key. Before and since, they have been known by other names – 'spiral step patterns', 'maze patterns', 'Celtic fret patterns', and so on – but 'key patterns', or 'keys' for short, is the most common and the name has a certain ring to it.

Key patterns, however, arrived late in the development of Celtic art. They appear to have entered the vocabulary of the Celtic artist/craftsman around the sixth century AD. They were probably developed by the scribes from decorations in the imported manuscripts that they were copying from, and then later used in metalwork, enamels, carved monuments and High Crosses. Key patterns lived only briefly compared to most Celtic motifs, disappearing again within three centuries under the tide of portraiture and primitive realism, as the cultural power of Charles the Great and the Roman church spread across Europe.

Nowadays there are very few books on Celtic art, and more specifically key patterns, which do not tell you that 'Celtic' is not the right word, and that it should be 'Pictish'. There are other terms used for the style that reached its peak in the stunningly decorated manuscripts of the seventh and eighth centuries – 'Hiberno-Saxon' (meaning 'from Scotland and northern England'), 'insular' (meaning 'from the British Isles') or 'Northumbrian' (basically referring to those manuscripts from the island of Lindisfarne and the Wearmouth-Jarrow monasteries, but often used more broadly). In this book I shall use the word 'Celtic', as it is the most widely used and because the Picts did not live in Ireland or Wales, where there is a well-documented wealth of artefacts decorated with key patterns.

Finding out about the Picts, however, is rather harder. To paraphrase one archaeologist, 'We can't say conclusively that we have found any Pictish remains as we have never found anything that is exclusively Pictish'. This is because the Picts were really just another Celtic tribe. There were hundreds, if not thousands, of them all across Europe before the expansion of the Roman empire, and their culture was very similar throughout. The only real difference that we can see now is that the developments in the culture seem to have spread slowly from the east to the west, taking a century or two to travel from eastern Europe to the Western Isles. As the Romans moved further north and west, the Celtic tribes were pushed before them, until the unconquered lands – Cornwall, Wales, Scotland, Ireland and, to a lesser extent, Brittany, were the only strongholds of Celtic culture left. In fact, the Romans did such a good job in wiping out all the cultures that they met that Ireland was the centre for education in western Europe for centuries to come.

The Celts of Ireland and northern Britain certainly took the elements of their traditional art and combined it with some of the elements of Byzantine art to create a new and beautiful hybrid. It is mainly due to the popularity of these manuscripts that we see this style as Celtic, rather than the style that for a thousand years and more led up to them. The classic Celtic style was based on long, flowing curves and a huge repertoire of spirals and animal designs. The rigid design elements were brought in with Christianity from the East, with the manuscript Bibles that the Celtic Christians of the sixth century onwards copied. From what we have left to study, it would appear that it did not take long for a synthesis of the two styles to develop. It may well be that this was because the same craftsmen and craftswomen who had already learnt the style of their ancestors for other uses – carving, body-painting, metalwork and jewellery – were recruited as scribes. The similarities between the illuminated manuscripts and contemporary jewellery must be more than a coincidence. If you want to find out more about the history of Celtic art and manuscripts visit my web site at http://www. net-shopper.co.uk/creative/.

Whatever you are planning to decorate with key patterns, this book should help you understand the basics and all the major variations. There are not as many possibilities as there are for Celtic knotwork, but they certainly number in the hundreds, many of which have never been drawn. As in my previous book, *How to Draw Celtic Knotwork*, I have tried to show a completely different approach to the manuals previously published. This is deliberate, as the aim is to show that by looking at key patterns (or anything else) from a different perspective, whole new vistas appear.

Key patterns are just another variation on that most loved of Celtic designs – the spiral. Of course, they are made of straight lines and triangles, and look nothing like traditional Celtic spirals, but that is what they are.

The S-curve ⌐ (so-called for obvious reasons) was one of the more common Celtic spiral elements. If you take a lot of S-curves, you can link and repeat them *ad nauseam*.

⌐ԼլԸլԸլԸլԸլԸլԸլԸլԸլԸլԸլԸլԸլԸլԸլԸլԸլԸլԸլԸլ ⌐

The way to draw a spiral is to start by drawing a series of concentric circles, increasing in size by regular amounts. Mark off a point on the innermost circle, move around by 90° and mark off a point on the next circle. Keep repeating this until you get to the outermost circle, then join up the points with a simple curve.

The basic key pattern is drawn the same way, but with straight lines. Start at a central point, and draw a straight line 1 unit long. Then rotate by 90° and draw a straight line 2 units long, rotate by 90°, draw a straight line 3 units long, and so on.

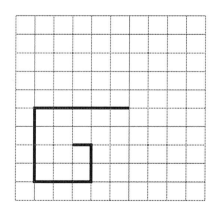

To make it into a key pattern (or to make the spiral an S-curve), simply copy the spiral, rotate it by 180° and stick the 2 ends together.

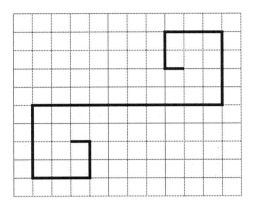

Unfortunately, this is not quite right, because what has just been made is a typical classical fret pattern, and the difference is this: with the fret, if you repeat them as we did with the S-curve, you get a basic diagonal single line border:

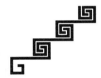

Which, while it may look nice, is not quite Celtic. It does repeat to form an interlinked block, but the edges do not lend themselves to embellishment the way that key patterns do.

Almost exclusively, key patterns were used to decorate borders or blocks; so they needed to repeat horizontally or vertically. It was a simple move, therefore, to rotate the whole design through 45° to fix this. So developed the distinctive Celtic variation of one of the most widespread forms of decoration;

Key patterns differ from classical fret not only by this change of angle. This small change leads to a wealth of embellishment, creating a much greater library of designs than any other culture managed before or since with fret patterns. As in the science of fractals, a small change can make a huge difference.

There is a tradition in art history from the nineteenth century, which some still hold to be true, that all real art in Europe developed from Roman and Greek art, and that before the Romans came to Britain there was no indigenous art form. Therefore Celtic key patterns must have developed from classical fret patterns, brought to the area by traders, although of course this ignores the archaeological evidence of widespread trading in prehistoric times. This may be the case. The same argument could be used to claim that key patterns came from the Chinese, as there is archaeological evidence of indirect trade with China. It could also be argued that the Celts developed their art forms from a slightly different branch of the same basic geometry. After all the British Museum has an Egyptian carving showing a key pattern panel from around 3000 BC and there are mammoth tusks from the Ukraine carved with key patterns from 15,000 BC.

Surely it is not the ancestry of such patterns that is important, but the fact that the necessary change was made, enabling a completely different-looking series of patterns to be drawn. As far as I know it was the Picts, Celts from the north of Scotland, who developed these particular patterns, explored their possibilities and left us a rich collection, showing us the possibilities of the key pattern. And to take it one small step further, it is not where, when and by whom they were discovered; the important thing is what you can do with them. And the better you understand them, the more that you can do with them, so on with the numbers.

NUMBERS

As we have seen, key patterns are just simple S-curve spirals made with straight lines. The numbers to describe them are just as simple.

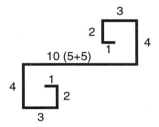

We'll start with one of the most basic key patterns to make things even simpler.

The first line is 1 unit long. The second must be 2 units long so that there is a gap of 1 unit on either side of the interlocking key.

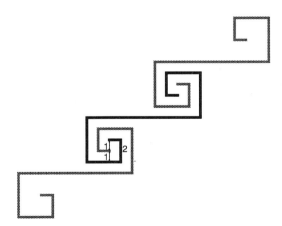

The third line must be 2 units longer than the first for the same reason.

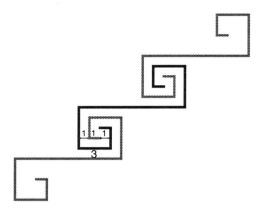

The fourth must be 2 units longer than the second for the same reason, and so on.

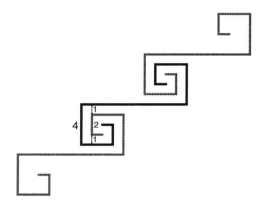

In this case the fourth line is the 'backbone' of the key, joining the 2 symmetrical spirals on either end. By looking at the pattern you can see that the length of the line is the length of the second line of the key, plus the length of the third line in the next key, plus the ubiquitous 2 to separate the keys.

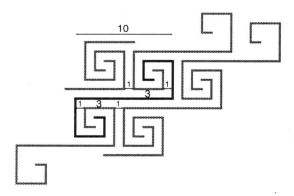

To simplify this we can write it as a basic formula, where x is the length of the first line and y is the length of the second line:

x, y, $x+2$, $y+2$, $x+4$, $y+4$, $x+6$, $y+6$, and so on, until the 'backbone', which is $(x+a)+(y+b)+2$ i.e. two units longer than the two previous lengths added together.

And it gets simpler. The second line must always be 2 units long in order to separate it from the last line of the interlocking key.

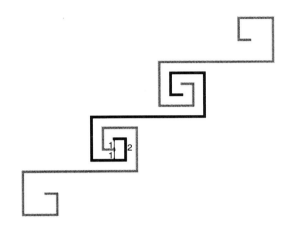

So in the above equation $y = 2$, so it can be rewritten x, 2, $x+2$, 4, $x+4$, 6, $x+6$, 8 and so on.

The first 7 key patterns that this gives for $x = 1$ and $x = 2$ are

1,2,5	2,2,6
1,2,3,7	2,2,4,8
1,2,3,4,9	2,2,4,4,10
1,2,3,4,5,11	2,2,4,4,6,12
1,2,3,4,5,6,13	2,2,4,4,6,6,14
1,2,3,4,5,6,7,15	2,2,4,4,6,6,8,16

From this you should be able to see the pattern and create your own absurdly convoluted key patterns, if you so wish.

There is now just a single piece of information stopping you from using these keys. Remember that key patterns are repeat patterns; in other words, the same pattern is repeated to fill a larger area. What we need to know is how many units high and wide the pattern is. Of course the key itself is the repeating pattern, but for our purposes (actually fitting the keys into an area), it will be far simpler to find a square or rectangular section that will repeat itself horizontally and vertically.

The number of units needed for the pattern to repeat itself horizontally and vertically for each of the above patterns are as follows:

key	horizontal	vertical	key	horizontal	vertical
1,2,5	6	6	2,2,6	5	3
1,2,3,7	20	4	2,2,4,8	25	5
1,2,3,4,9	15	5	2,2,4,4,10	7	5
1,2,3,4,5,11	25	6	2,2,4,4,6,12	49	7
1,2,3,4,5,6,13	28	7	2,2,4,4,6,6,14	9	7
1,2,3,4,5,6,7,15	72	8	2,2,4,4,6,6,8,16	81	9
1,2,3,4,5,6,7,8,17	45	9	2,2,4,4,6,6,8,8,18	11	9

So now that we have understood the basic geometry of key patterns, it is time to find out about drawing them.

REPEAT SECTIONS

Key patterns are, to state the blindingly obvious, made of sections of the same pattern repeated over and over to fill an area. To work out what size the repeated section is, all you have to do is to measure from a specific point on a key to the same point on the next key vertically and horizontally. For instance:

Then using these as the height and width, we can draw a rectangle enclosing part of the overall key pattern:

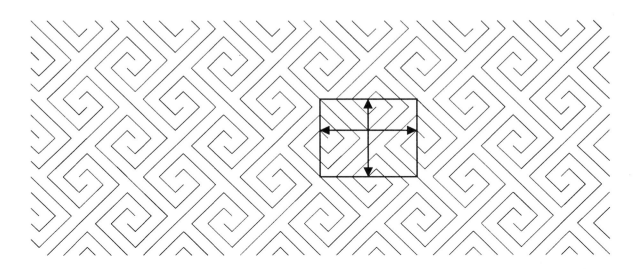

This can then be extracted and repeated vertically and horizontally to create the endless key pattern that we are looking for:

Brought together they look like this, which is what we were after.

This does produce a complete fill pattern in its own right, though they still do not have the distinctive Celtic feel to them. In order to make complete key patterns, with their edges and corners, we need rather more sections than just this. If you imagine a complete key pattern as a 3 by 3 square or rectangle, then what we have is merely the central section. What we must now do is learn how to finish off the pattern by creating the other 8 sections.

These rectangular sections are what are illustrated at the end of this book in the **Sections** chapter (page 91).

CREATING THE CORNERS AND EDGES

So far we have only been learning to draw the keys themselves, in fact, only the central repeat section. You can fill an area just using these sections, but there are two problems: first, there are no examples of a key pattern being drawn or carved this way in traditional Celtic art, although this in itself should not stop you experimenting with it. Much more importantly it is just plain messy. Traditionally there are two ways of finishing off the edges: the easy way and the not-so-easy way.

The first, and simplest, method is to block off the edges with filled-in solid triangles, leaving only full and half key patterns.

This gives a series of 'teeth' along the edge and large triangles at all four of the corners. These large triangles are traditionally broken up with a 'lozenge' shape, as in the example above, to provide a bit of extra interest, as well as to break the large triangles into a size closer to the teeth along the edge. These lozenges had been used for well over a thousand years by the Celts, to divide up large solid areas (such as in spirals), before the development of key patterns in the manuscripts.

You may notice that in this version, the bottom left-hand corner is not very neat, because it has cut part of the key spiral off. To correct this problem, the triangles can be made slightly smaller. If you made just the one corner smaller it would look rather strange. Therefore all of the triangles must be made smaller in order to even and neaten everything up.

But look, what have we here? Exactly the same problem all over again. But if we do the same again, not only does it get a fraction shorter, but it looks even worse, with blocked-off sections along the edge.

The way to make it look right is to go back to the second variation and take out the lozenges. This way the different sizes of the triangled corners is rather less obvious and when you draw it, the chances are that it will only be you who notices the problem, if indeed you think it is a problem, rather than a solution.

This method only really works in a few of the possible key patterns, such as the following 12349 key, to be found in the Book of Lindisfarne, where this form of edging is particularly common.

This style is not shown in the Sections chapter at the end of the book (page 91). If you want to draw key patterns in this style, you will have to work out what looks best to you, which should, hopefully, not be too hard.

So, to fit in with their sense of style, a different way had to be found, and this is what the Celts came up with:

In this version the opposite corners are always symmetrical, unlike the toothed edges that we have just been looking at. Going from one to the other is not the most obvious step, I grant you, but it definitely has style, and what is now called 'design value'. So how do we get to this from the overall pattern?

The best place for us to start in order to achieve this is at the corners.

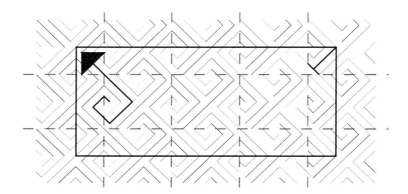

As you can see, the top right-hand corner is measured from the end of the longest line of the spiral part of the key, where it meets the 'backbone' of the key.

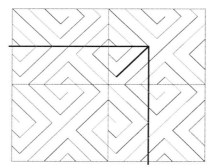

The opposite corner is the same, and from these you can draw the box to frame the pattern.

Now ink in the same line in each of the repeat sections. These are the 'branches' that connect the key pattern to the frame.

Next, the '1 unit away' rule comes into play again. If we draw another rectangle inside the first, these are the vertical and horizontal lines for the bases of the edge triangles.

There is now a series of lines which, now that they have been cut off by the inner rectangle, form right-angled triangles with one side vertical or horizontal. Ink these in.

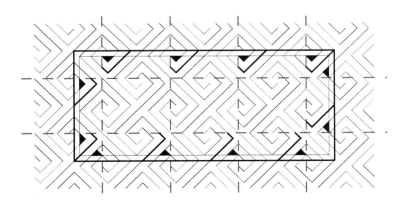

The edge patterns are all identical, so the large triangles must be added to the sides with the small ones, and vice versa.

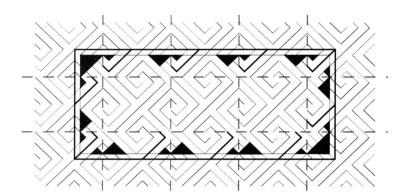

Note that in this particular case there are 2 branches connecting the pattern to the frame along the top. The edges do not have to be symmetrical top and bottom or side to side; it is unusual, but not unheard of. As with all key patterns, the geometry of the design is paramount and the artist is hardly left to improvise at all. Where there is room for experimentation, it is severely limited by the overall style. After all, unlike other Celtic design elements such as knotwork and spirals, key patterns are based entirely on straight lines, not the most common element of traditional (i.e. pre-Christian) Celtic art.

So now it is time to ink in all the keys.

On removing the guide pattern you will see that there are a few gaps in the pattern around the edges. These can now be added, following the '1 unit away' rule. To provide at least a small degree of possible variation for the artist to experiment with, this can be done in either of two ways: first, the more common form, where the gaps are filled by a line 1 unit long, coming from the corner of the key pattern, forming a T-junction:

Secondly, the less common form, where the line comes from the top of the small triangle. Look how this changes the line at the corners and you will see why it is rarely, if ever, seen in traditional Celtic designs. The single straight lines along the top and 3 lines ending together are not part of the usual Celtic repertoire:

DRAWING THE PATTERNS

Now that we understand the basics of key patterns, we may as well learn how to draw them. The first thing we start with is the area that we want to fill. As key patterns are almost always used to fill an area with decoration, the area that they need to fill is usually defined before starting to draw. In my experience, the illustrations in this book are the first time I have had to start with the pattern rather than the area. This is why I have tried to include a variety of proportions in the repeats in the Sections chapter (page 91), so that most areas will be fillable by one or more of them.

So we start with an area which, in the case of this example, will be four by three, the classic Pictish proportions.

Next we divide up each of these squares into an equal number of smaller boxes. This number can be just about anything, but 4 or fewer is generally too small, and the more you have, the more complex the pattern. In this example we will divide them by 8, giving us a rectangle of 32 by 24.

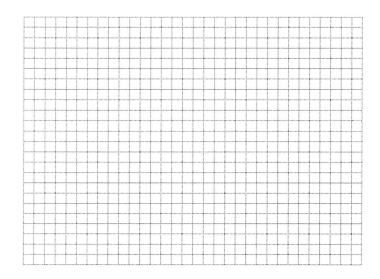

As we have seen, the corners are always formed the same way, so we may as well start with them. All you have to do is decide which corner is to be which, and what size to make the large triangle. In this case we will have the large triangle corner in the top right (and bottom left) and the 'branch' corner in the top left (and bottom right), and the horizontal and vertical sides of the triangles will be four units long.

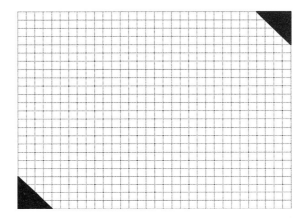

The corners, as we have seen, are merely the triangles from the horizontal and vertical edges put together, so by cutting the large corner triangle in half we get the triangles that are repeated along the edges.

This takes us to our next step – deciding on the size of our repeats. We are now left with an area of 24 by 16. The length could be divided into repeats of 4, 6, 8 or 12, while the height can only be divided into repeats of 4 or 8. To keep it basic we will divide up the area, both horizontally and vertically into repeats of 8, giving ourselves a square repeat pattern.

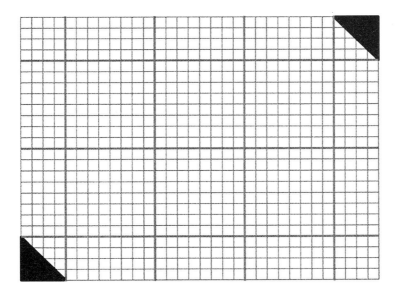

In general it is best to keep the repeats as close to a square as the numbers allow, as this gives the more traditional key patterns. The greater the difference between the height and width, the harder it is to work out a pattern to fill it, and the more likely that there is no key that could fill it. To see why this is, we must understand that the diagonal nature of key patterns, and that the 'backbone' of the key forces the repeat to be almost square. The exception to this is when a key does not quite repeat itself horizontally.

A lot of keys move up or down 1 unit when repeated so, to get a proper horizontal repeatable section, the key must be repeated until it is on the same level as it started. For instance, if it drops 1 unit with each return and the vertical repeat is 8 units, then the key must be repeated 8 times before it is on the same level as it started.

But to get back to drawing our 8 by 8 pattern. We have seen before that the large corner triangle is just the vertical and horizontal triangles from the repeats stuck together, so we can now use this the other way. By cutting the large triangle in half we get the vertical and horizontal border triangles, which we can now place in the same position in each of the repeated edge sections. In other words, as the large triangle is in the top right-hand corner of the pattern, it meets the left-hand edge of the repeated sections along the top and the bottom edge of the repeated sections along the right. The other sides are exactly the opposite.

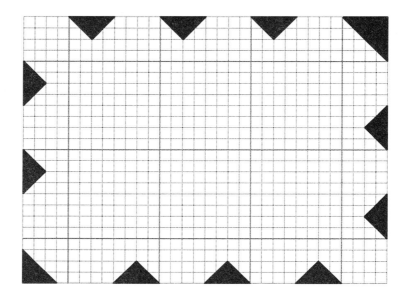

The other thing that we know about the large corner triangles is that they are on the end of the 'backbone'; so we can now add these into each of the repeated edge sections:

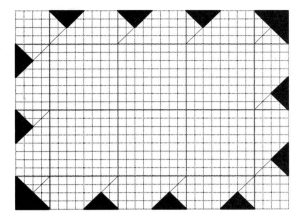

Now it is time to work out the other 2 corners. We know that there is a 'branch' line coming in diagonally from the corner, as there is in all key patterns. Using the '1 unit away' rule, we know where the 'branch' ends and, once we have drawn it in, we can see which other points must have lines going to them.

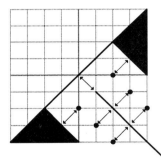

And so, as with most other key pattern corners, the end of the 'branch' can be made into a T-junction, and 2 smaller triangles can be joined to the larger ones.

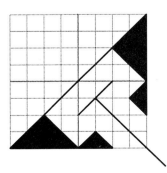

These smaller triangles and the 'branch' can now be repeated throughout the pattern, completing the edges.

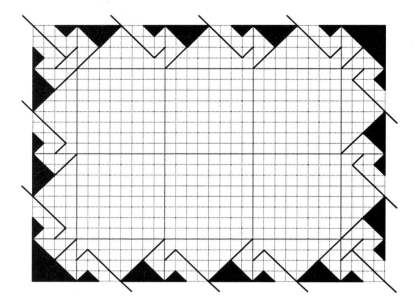

But there is a problem with this – the 'branches' touch the triangles along the edges. The only way to solve this is to chop the corners off the triangles like this:

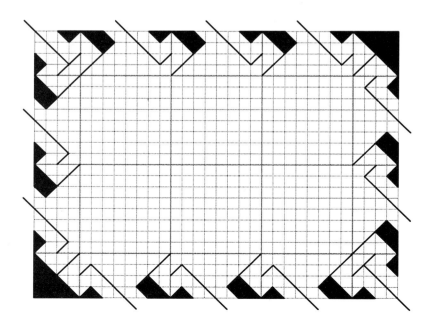

So we now have the edges sorted out, so it is time to fill in the middle. This is done in much the same way, because, as we saw earlier, the edges are just cut-down versions of the larger central repeat section. So to start we simply copy the 'branches' to the same position in the central sections.

First with the top and bottom 'branches', which meet up to form the 'backbones' of the keys.

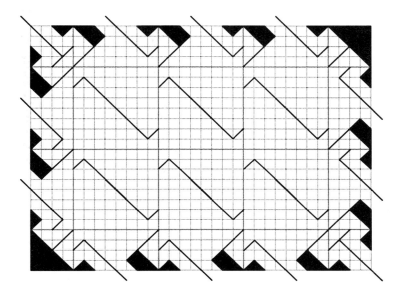

And next with the 'backbones' from either side, which are extended until they are 1 unit away from the lines that we have just drawn.

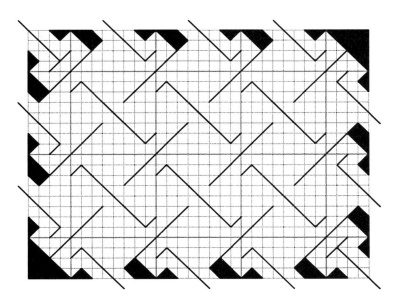

These lines do not give us any idea of which way they turn at their ends, but we will come to that soon, as what we have so far gives us a very solid base from which to build up the complete keys.

The first step is to extend the short lines from the copied 'branches' until they are (you guessed it) 1 unit away from the next line. Note that the 'branches' along the right- and left-hand edges have to be made into T-junctions, and the new lines extended so that they make similar lines in their sections.

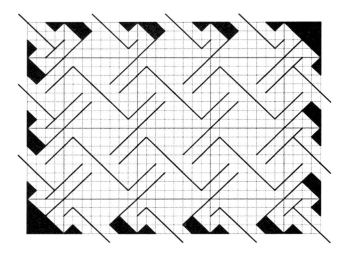

Now we have to turn a corner, and there is only one way to go. So we draw these lines until they too are 1 unit away from the next lines they would meet. We would keep this up, always turning in the same direction (not that there is an alternative) until the last lines are only 1 unit long. These have to be the ends of the keys. But in this case the lines that we have just drawn are only 1 unit long, so this is the key finished.

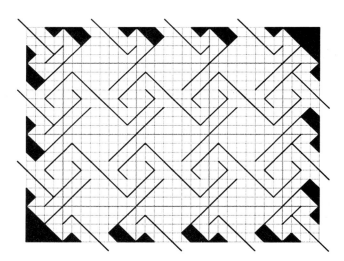

Now we have to create the keys that go the other way, the ones made from the extended 'backbones'. This is just as straightforward, as there are really no alternatives here either. So first we turn a corner and draw a line from the end of the 'backbone' to 1 unit away from the next 'backbone'. Note that along the top and bottom edges, these lines have to emerge from the tetrahedra (the triangles with their corners cut off) in order to fit in with the repeat pattern in the other sections.

The previous steps are then repeated to make the completed pattern.

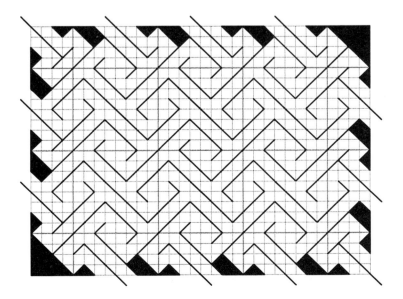

So there we have the complete pattern. All that is left to do is make the outside border, by drawing lines along the ends of the 'branches' and it is all done.

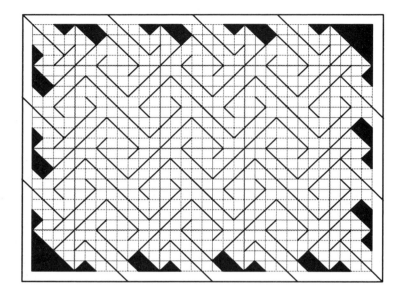

But wait a minute, I hear you say: what about the '1 unit away' rule? The ends of the keys are 2 units apart with no obvious way of bringing them closer. In fact, this is not a problem, and is found fairly frequently in traditional key patterns. The Celts, with their usual ingenuity, found several ways of dealing with this, and we will be looking at them in later chapters.

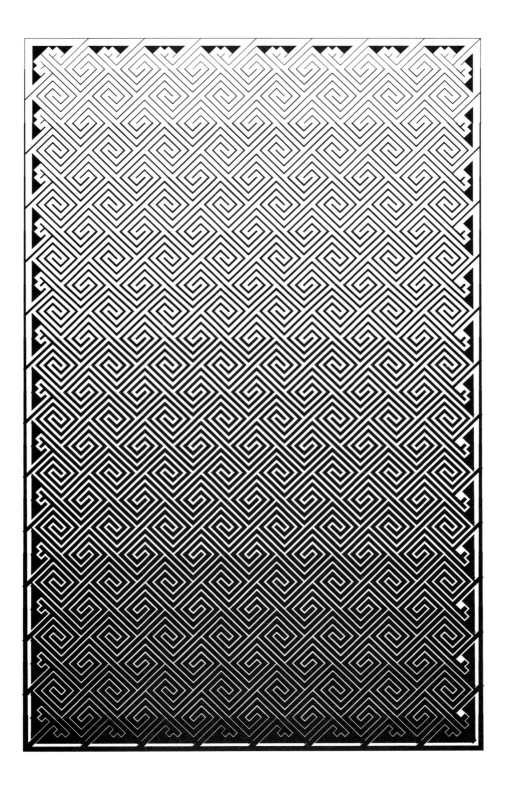

THICKENING THE LINES

So far we have only dealt with key patterns in their thin line form. Traditionally, more often than not, they were drawn in their thick line form.

thin   thick

This brings out the balance in the pattern as the background has now become a pattern of lines of equal thickness to the lines of the keys. Usually the keys are drawn or painted in a dark colour, almost invariably black, while the background is in a much lighter colour.

This enhances the balance for the viewer because, when drawn the other way round, with the keys lighter, the background pattern is less noticable.

The method of converting from the thin line version to the thick was simple for the illuminators of the great Celtic manuscripts; they just used a quill that had been cut so that it was half a unit wide. It is not quite so simple for those of us who do not make our own pens, but it is still fairly easy.

Just draw a new line around 1 thin line, $\frac{1}{4}$ of a unit away on each side, making the line into an area $\frac{1}{2}$ a unit wide.

Now fill in this area.

The other lines become the background line, so can be erased.

ANOTHER VARIATION

There is a second way of thickening the lines which creates a pattern that looks very different.

This variation gives the rarer form of key pattern, although it is the form that gave the pattern its name – the key. In line with being described as an S-curve, this can be described as a J-curve or a y-curve.

The patterns are intriguing because at first they look very similar to the S-curve, but the more you study them the harder it is to see the connection. This connection is very simple – 1 line 1 unit long.

Drawing them is as easy as drawing S-curves. First draw your basic thin line key in pencil:

Next join the ends of the S-curves together with a line 1 unit long, as always:

Starting in the middle of the design, ink in a line, as you did when thickening the lines, $\frac{1}{4}$ of a unit away from each pencil line:

Note how, on the outside edges of the blocks, the line is drawn over the pencil line rather than $\frac{1}{4}$ of a unit away from it:

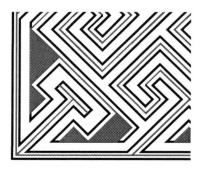

If you now fill the pattern in as you did when thickening the lines, you get the following, which still does not look like an obvious y-curve pattern:

This can be changed to a more obvious y-curve by colouring in the background, rather than the foreground, which brings out the pattern. This variation also, uniquely, has the blocks as part of the background, rather than the foreground:

You will notice that in these patterns, unlike the other variations, there is a solid line going from one side of the pattern to the other:

CREATING KEY BORDERS

Now we come to probably the most common use of key patterns – narrow borders. These are to be found in just about every Celtic manuscript in existence, and most likely in the hundreds that have been destroyed or lost. Even the most primitive of the manuscripts – such as the Book of Deer – which contain little of the decoration we think of as Celtic, still have key pattern borders.

These make the greatest use of the Celtic edging, as they consist of little other than top and bottom edges put together.

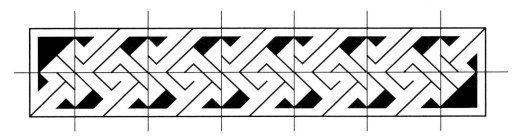

If you are using the sections at the end of this book (see page 91), it is a simple matter of just copying the sections on the top row, then adding those from the bottom row.

If, however, you want to create them from scratch, there are other ways to do it. For all of them you need to start with a grid to draw in. The grid needed to draw the above pattern is 50 by 10, although of course you would generally be starting with a predetermined grid of a certain size, and working out a pattern to fill it, rather than the other way round as we are doing here.

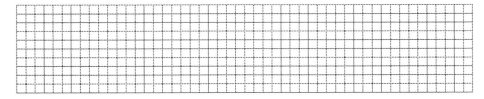

Now we need to divide this grid up into equal, repeated sections. First we take away the corners, the size of which we know. We know this because the corner sections are always square, we know that the height of the border is 10 units, so each corner must be a 5 by 5 square.

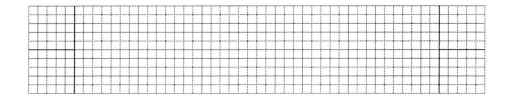

This leaves us with 40 units to divide up equally. We could choose 4, 5, 8, 16 or 20, each could produce a wealth of varieties, but in this case, once again, we will divide it up into repeats of 8 units.

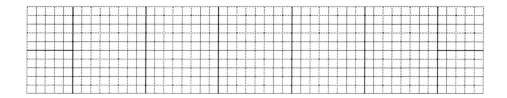

Next we take off 1 unit all around each edge for the horizontal and vertical edges of the triangles.

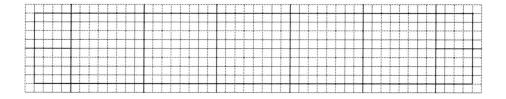

From here we can go either of 2 ways. We can either start with the edges and work in or we can start at the centre of each section and work outwards to the edges. The most common method is to start at the centre so, just to be perverse, as usual, I will start by showing the method that starts at the edges.

When we start drawing the pattern it is simplest to start off with the corners again. With a 5 by 5 section, there are 4 possible variations for the 'triangle' corners: with horizontal and vertical sides 2 or 4 units long. 1- and 3-unit long sides do not work as they clash with the '1 unit away' rule. The central diagonal line coming from the triangle would, at some point, be $\frac{1}{2}$ a unit or $1\frac{1}{2}$ units away from the adjoining triangles.

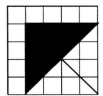 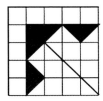 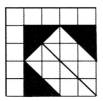 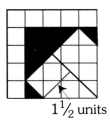

$1\frac{1}{2}$ units

In this case we will use the 2-unit long version, and from this we can work out the 'branch' corners at the same time.

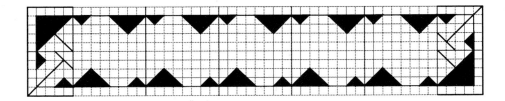

The next step is to take the small triangle and half of the large corner triangle and copy them in the same position, i.e. against the right-hand edges and the left-hand edges along the bottom and top of each section, like so:

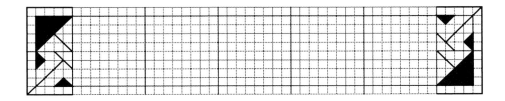

What you should notice here is that the gap between the small and large triangles that we have just drawn is 2 horizontal units. As we have seen previously, the horizontal gap between any 2 diagonal lines must be 2 units in order to keep the lines 1 diagonal unit apart. Into this gap we have to fit the diagonal 'branch' line that connects the key pattern to the border. We must, therefore, lop something off. We could take out the small triangle, but in this case we will take 1 corner off the larger triangle. This leaves us with a gap of 4 units, and into the middle of this we can put the 'branch'.

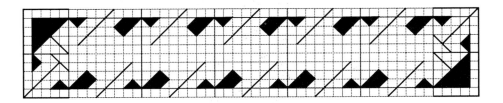

If you look at the top left and bottom right corners there is an obvious line, 1 unit long, needed to fill the gap. This can be added to all the 'branch' lines.

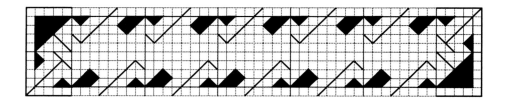

Looking at the opposite corners, there are 2 lines which point to the corner of the block on the opposite side. If you connect these up, and do it for all the other repeats as well, the S-curve shape becomes more visible. In this case, because both are edges, they are closer to Zs than Ss, but you get the idea.

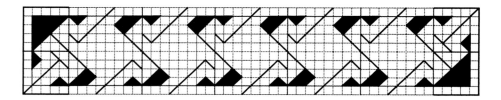

This leaves us with a nice square to fill in with lines that spiral inwards, always staying 1 unit apart. These lines could start at any of 3 sets of points: the other free corner of the edge block, by making a T-junction at the end of the 'branch', or by using one of each. However if we use both the T-junctions we get the following pattern, which breaks the '1 unit apart' rule with the gaps between the ends, which is 2 diagonal units, not 1.

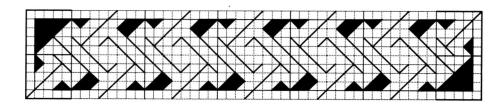

And by starting with the free corners of the edge blocks we get the following, which does not work for exactly the same reasons:

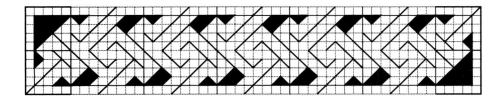

Finally, if we try one of each, we find we get this pattern, which works perfectly.

The pattern that we have just created could have been altered in several ways at different points in its construction, and can be further varied from here, as the next chapters will show. To a large extent, however, as the last step has shown us, the pattern is defined mainly by the space it has to fill and the '1 step away' rule.

MAKING OTHER VARIATIONS

As has been mentioned several times in this book already, one of the hallmarks of Celtic art throughout its long history was the constant experimentation with, and embellishment of, basic design elements. Unlike most of the Celts other favourite decorations, key patterns do not lend themselves easily to freehand improvisation. There is, of course, a very good reason for this and this is that, unlike all other traditional Celtic designs, the key patterns that developed with the coming of Christianity are made up exclusively of straight lines.

This does not mean that the scribes' natural tendency to experiment and innovate was wasted on keys. Apart from the development of the distinct edging that was discovered, there grew a wide variety of ways of finishing off the central spiral elements of the keys. Without changing the overall look of the key patterns, the lines of the central square (or rectangular) spiral can be joined, as we saw in the previous chapter, shortened, or embellished with triangles, rectangles or even circular spirals. The entire pattern can be made up of the edge sections reflected and repeated, or of the corner sections joined and repeated to fill an area.

All of these were drawn in the great illuminated manuscripts and carved on stone monuments that still exist today. And yet there are always more ways to be found to create a new and unique pattern. The more you play with key patterns, the more you will find.

TRIANGULATING THE ENDS

The first and most common variation is where the ends of the keys are filled with right-angled triangles which mirror those around the edges. They can come in several sizes, depending on the shape of the key pattern.

The first one is made with the smallest triangle, having 2 of its sides 1 unit long. To make this all you have to do is draw a line from the end of the key to a point 1 unit along the second line of each key:

Now it is just a case of filling in the triangle formed and there you have it.

The next variation is very similar, but with a slightly larger triangle. This time it goes from the end of the key to a point 2 units down the second line, which in this case is at the second corner.

The just fill the triangles in as before.

At this point a slight problem appears. At this angle the triangles are too close to conform to the '1 unit away' rule. At the scale at which the scribes drew their key patterns (i.e. tiny), this did not matter much but, for absolute accuracy, something must be done. One tried and tested method is to move the furthest point of the triangle back a way down the second line like so:

Unfortunately this does not work, as the 2 triangles are still less than 1 unit apart. They only become correct when you have brought the point a whole unit down the line, which takes us back to our previous small triangle.

The only way to make the triangles exactly 1 unit apart is to shorten the end line of the key.

However, the geometry required to calculate just how long the line must now be is much too complicated for our current task. Remember, we are just drawing patterns, not working on quantum mechanics, so the best way to make it look right is to do it by eye. If it looks right, it is right.

This style of variation can be extended as far as you like, taking the end of the triangle as far as the last corner of the spiral, where it meets the 'backbone' of the key although, as you can see, the first line is now deleted altogether and the second line must be shortened by about 1 unit in order to keep the triangles 1 unit away from each other. It is up to you to experiment to find the pattern that you want.

FLAGGING THE ENDS

The next variation, again a common one, is very similar to the last except that, instead of triangles, the central spiral lines are replaced by rectangles.

With these, for the first time, $\frac{1}{2}$ unit measurements are needed in order to keep the rectangles 1 unit apart. If the third line of the key is 3 units long, as they frequently are, the rectangles must be $\frac{1}{2}$ a unit wide, so that a 3 unit gap plus 2 $\frac{1}{2}$-unit-wide rectangles make up the 4 units of the length.

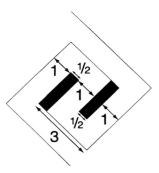

As with the triangles, the rectangles can be increased in size until they meet the 'backbone' of the key.

SPIRALLING THE ENDS

In spite of the fact that key patterns consist of straight lines and nothing else, there are examples of patterns where the two ends of each key spiral round each other. These were Celts, after all, and they had been perfecting spirals for well over a thousand years. There must have been hundreds of the artifacts found from the beginnings to the final corruption of Celtic art, many with unique variations on two-line spirals, which can be studied for inspiration. But it is much too large a subject to do justice to here. They did not often use the single-centred basic spirals that we think of today, but had a huge repertoire of decorative elements to work with. There were 'lenses', 'bracketed lozenges', 'duck's heads', and many more, which the Celts combined to beautiful effect.

The spirals in the design below are all from a shield mount found in Balmaclellan, south-west Scotland. This dates from at least 500, if not 1000, years before key patterns were used in the manuscripts, but it serves to show a minute fraction of the possibilities already shown, let alone the ones you can come up with.

We will not go into the geometry of spirals here, but merely point out that the best way to draw small spirals has to be by *eye* around a central point or points.

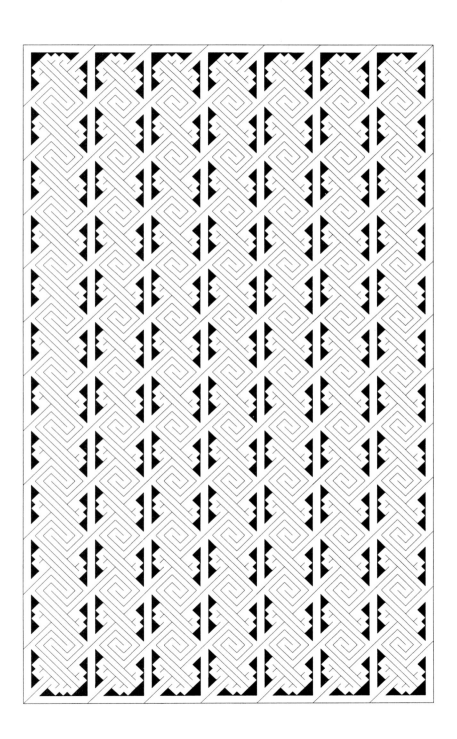

MIRRORING THE EDGES

If it is the edges that give these key patterns their Celtic feel, then this variation takes it one step further. This variation, done to a huge range of different keys, is found just about everywhere that key patterns are found. The reason is obvious – they are very easy to make. This may be one reason for their popularity, because the time in which key patterns were popular was the time that the skills and understanding needed for Celtic art were being lost. The basic knowledge of how to create the full key patterns may have been lost, but creating a new pattern from the edges of another is still easy. There is another reason for their popularity, which is that the dimensions of the sections change when this is done to a key pattern, allowing the pattern to be used in areas of different proportions.

When we learned to draw overall key patterns by hand we started by completing the edge sections before working out the central section. In this variation we never need get as far as the central section – although we do have to draw some spirals – as it consists of making a central section out of the two edges. So we will look at the pattern that we learned on, starting at the point when all the edges were completed.

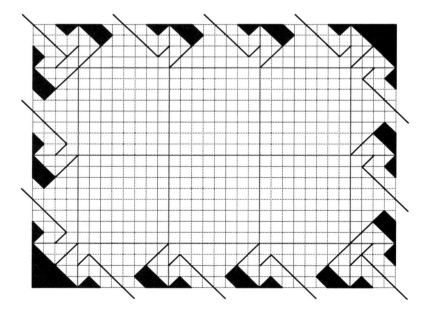

The first thing we have to do is decide whether we want the pattern to look vertical or horizontal. In this case, since the previous page has a vertical pattern, we will make it look horizontal. The difference is this: for the pattern to look vertical, we use the left and right edges for the central repeat, while to make it look horizontal we use the top and bottom edges. So our first step is to copy the top edge sections into the bottom of each central section, like so:

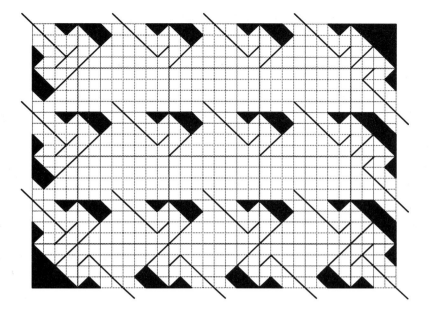

The next step is to copy the bottom edge sections into the top of each central section, like this, but as you can see this does not look very much like the edge sections repeated. This is because the triangles are touching, and if the pattern were to be completed it would look unlike any key pattern drawn before.

What we need to do is add an extra vertical unit to the central sections, making them 8 by 9 rather than 8 by 8, to separate the edges. This means that we also have to add an extra unit in the central left- and right-hand edge sections so that they repeat at the same rate as the central sections. This we can do by making the tetrahedra back into triangles again. In order to do this, we must bring the horizontal and vertical edges in by 1 unit.

This makes the 'branches' meet when put back to back. Previously the edge sections, including the 'branches', were 5 units high. To make them repeat in an 8 by 8 square, 1 unit must be shaved off each. Unfortunately, this does give us a series of corner 'branches' around the edges which go nowhere and, as you will see, it does not give us the most beautiful end result, but one of the purposes of this exercise is to show that you can make these variations on any key patterns in some way or another. There is an almost infinite number of possibilities hidden in this most basic of geometries – it is just up to you to explore and discover them.

But back to the much simplified edge sections. Because the repeat is 8 units wide and the horizontal gap must be 2 units on either side of the 'branch', this leaves us with a horizontal base of 4 units which can be divided in 2 to make 2 triangles with bases of 2 units.

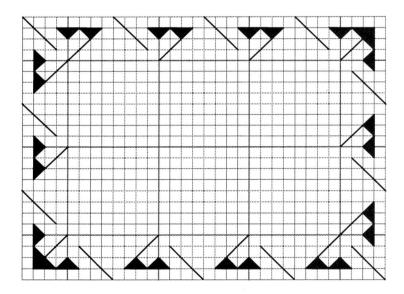

So now we start again with the top edge sections

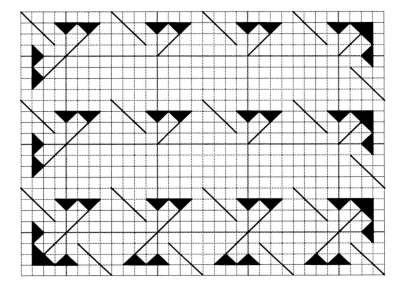

Then come the bottom sections along the tops of the central sections.

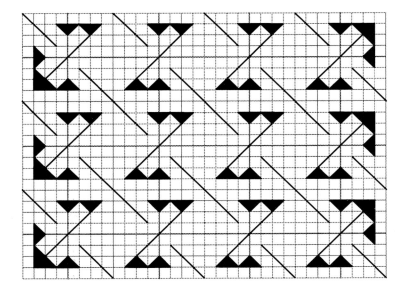

So now all there is left to do is draw in the spirals as we did before.

Or we can reflect the edge pattern that we had before, to make it a kind of double-edged pattern.

And, of course, there is another way of mirroring the keys, and this is to take the top 4 units of the pattern above and reflect them.

If we join the edge and its reflection then we get a thin border pattern.

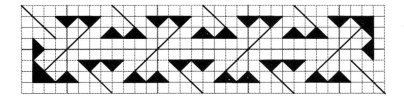

This can then be repeated endlessly to fill any area.

REPEATING THE MINIMUM KEY

This variation is just the logical extension of the last one. In that variation we used only the edge sections, while in this one we go one step further by only using the corner sections. This was often used for making small squares to be used as decoration.

Sometimes, however, it was used for filling larger areas. This is done simply by joining lots of them together.

And if we rotate or reflect every alternate square, we get a pretty 'snowflake' pattern.

There is a very limited number of corner variations, but they are all suitable for this treatment.

The minimum key square was also quite often used in a circular border as a very basic decoration.

FOUR-LINE SPIRALS

The four-line spiral or swastika was a common variation in the past, and as such is a major variation in its own right. The spirals differ fundamentally in that instead of using the S-curve, they use the H-curve, which is almost, but not quite, the S-curve reflected across its 'backbone'. The keys alternate in direction every column or row in just the same way as the S-curves do. The difference lies in the fact that the keys interlock with 4 others, rather than 2.

This also affects the maths in that, because the '1 unit away' rule still applies and there are now 4 lines, the length of the lines must increase by at least 2 each time, rather than 1. This pattern, for instance can be described as a 1,3,5,12 H-curve, while the next size up would be 1,3,5,7,16. The 'backbone' is the previous number plus 1, doubled. If the first line is an even number of units long (usually 2), then the ends of the lines opposite each other can be joined to form the classic swastika.

For this example we will be using the 1,3,5,12 H-curve, as there are more interesting things that can be done with the ends. This is a slightly different way of drawing key patterns, just to show that there are several ways to get to the end result. It is based on the idea that we know the key pattern we want, but not how the edges look.

Starting with the grid, which in this case is 28 by 28 (the size of the repeat section is 14 by 14), we first put in the corners. We have seen that the triangle corners have the 'backbone' coming out of them, so we can place them and their repeats.

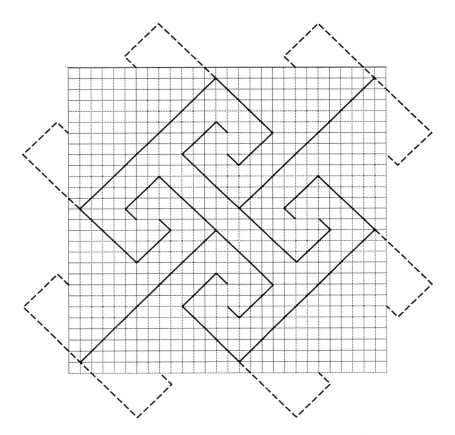

Notice that the lines should only be drawn up to a point 1 unit in from the edge of the grid. This is so that the edging triangles can be drawn attached to them, at whatever size will be needed to fill the spaces left when we have drawn in all the H-curve key pattern lines.

It should be fairly easy to see where the opposite H-curve goes, so we put this in and repeat it where needed.

Again all the lines are cut off 1 unit from the edge of the grid, except where the 'backbones' go out of the grid. As these are to become the 'branches' which connect to the outer frame, they are drawn up to the very edge of the grid.

The space that we have to fill with triangles is 8 units long. There are various ways to divide it, but we will use triangles with base lengths of 5 and 3. There are a few lines that need shortening at the corners, but as long as we follow the '1 unit away' rule it is all fairly straightforward. We can then decorate the centres of the spirals how ever we wish.

KEY PATTERN RINGS

Although there are not many examples of key pattern rings (technically known as 'annular' key patterns) left, this is one of the more attractive uses of key patterns, combining as it does, the straight lines of the key patterns with circles. All the lines curve slightly, but the overall effect is not lost. The sweeping curves of traditional Celtic art can be seen tugging at the rigid, relatively modern form of decoration.

They are, however, relatively easy to draw. It is best to start with an idea of what the key pattern you are going to use looks like as a straight line border.

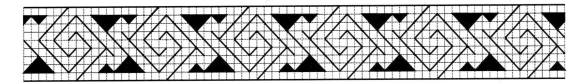

This border is made of the top and bottom central sections put together and then repeated 6 times. As the repeat section measures 10 by 12 the final border will measure 10 by 72 units.

So our first step is to draw the inner and outer circles and divide the area between into 9 concentric rings.

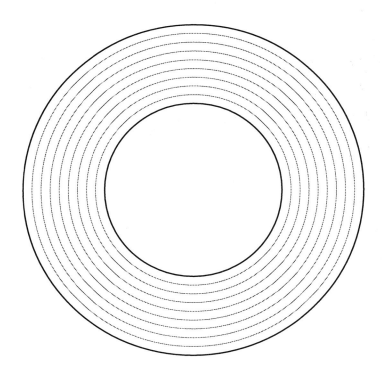

The next step is to divide the ring into 72 equal parts. A convenient number 72, as it divides neatly into the 360° of a circle 5 times. So we mark off the rings at 5° intervals.

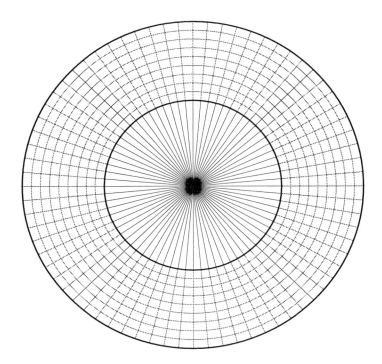

Now all we have to do is fill in the pattern. It is exactly the same as the straight line pattern above, only the units by which they are drawn have altered. First we will draw the triangles, as they give the quickest overview of the pattern. If we look at the bases of the triangles, their lengths are 4 units followed by 2 units, followed by a gap of 6 units. So we first draw the bases 6 units long then leave a gap of 6 units, and so on all the way around. If you are left with a gap that is too short or too long, check all the other lines and gaps and you will find the problem.

On the straight line version, the lower (inner) base lines start and finish 2 units to the right of the bases on the top. In the annular version, this is the equivalent of 2 units clockwise, so we can draw these in too. As you can see, the line curves with the circle, and this should be the same for all the lines in the pattern. In practice though, the shortest lines and the edges of the triangles will have a barely perceptible curve to them, which you can ignore or accentuate, depending on your mood and plans for the piece. Human pattern recognition works in such a way as to make the pattern more understandable as the lines are straightened, and more bizarre the more the lines curve. The final effect is up to you.

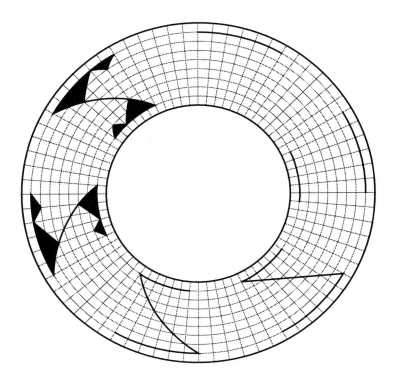

Next we can draw in the line that connects the base lines from the right-hand (clockwise) end to the left-hand (anticlockwise) end. Note that to fit into the units, the line has to curve slightly again, as do the sides of the triangles as we come to draw these in.

In the example, going clockwise, I have shown the straight line versions followed by the curved versions. These could be further curved, if so desired, to create an even more angular feel to the pattern. As you can see, the 'backbone' really must be curved if the units are to be of any use in helping to draw the rest of the pattern. Of course, having said that, I am the last person to tell you not to try out new variations. It would be going against the spirit of the style to refrain from experimenting.

But back to the ring. Once we have all the triangles drawn in, it is now time to put in the square spirals between them. Again we use the straight line border to work from. We start with the 'branches', which emerge from the border lines half way through the gap between the triangles. When drawing the square spirals that fill the gaps, it is always best to draw the lines alternately from the outside and inside of the ring. This way you can always see where the line that you are drawing should finish. These lines should theoretically mirror the curves of the 'backbones' that we just drew, but, again, they can be made to curve more or less, depending on the feel that you are aiming at.

And here we have the completed ring. Any of the variations shown in this book can be made to this pattern.

CIRCULAR KEY PATTERNS

There are two ways of drawing key patterns to fill circles, one very rare in traditional Celtic art, the other fairly common. Strangely, the easier of the two is hardly ever seen, while the more common is slightly more complex to draw and the end result is less obviously a key pattern.

We will draw the easier of the two first. As with all these variations, it is always best to have an idea of what the basic rectangular key pattern looks like. In this variation we are only going to need the central section, which we will bend to fit the circle.

Start with a circle with a square grid inside, centred on the centre of the circle. The number of units in the grid depends on which key pattern we are going to use, but in general it is best to have the width and/or height as a multiple of the section size.

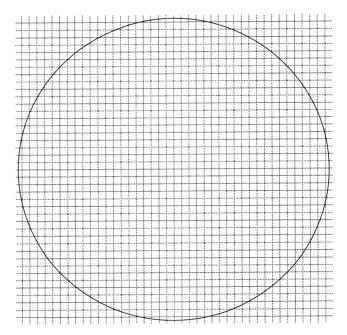

Now we just fill in the pattern, using repeats of the central section, starting at the centre of the circle, but stopping short of the edge by a unit or 2.

Now all we have to do is draw in the lines, as similarly as possible to the original, curving them so that the outer lines curve parallel to the outer circle.

Notice that the short lines that have been cut off should be turned into spirals to complete the S-curves.

This variation has very strong similarities to Chinese lattice work, but it should not be assumed that the Celts and Chinese had any contact, The pattern as drawn is a very basic geometrical design, which does not stand out as Celtic because it is not edged with the traditional triangles.

The simplicity of this method may be the reason that there are so few archaeological examples of this style. Much more common is the following method, which uses the geometry of the circle for its grid. Both variations have their advantages and disadvantages, as we will see. The choice is up to you when you draw your own. This one looks more Celtic, though many possible versions do not look much like key patterns. To make an even more Celtic-looking key circle, there may be ways to combine the formation of the outer edge of an annular pattern and the inside of the second way of forming a circular pattern. However, I have never seen one.

On to the second method of creating circular key patterns. Instead of using a square grid, this one uses a grid made up of lines radiating from the centre and concentric circles. For this example we mark off the radial lines at 6° intervals, so that there are 60 of them around the circle. This we can then divide into 6 wedges of 10 units, so we may as well use 10 units going the other way as well. It is best to add another unit for the centre of the circle because the radial lines are so close by now that they are impossible to work with.

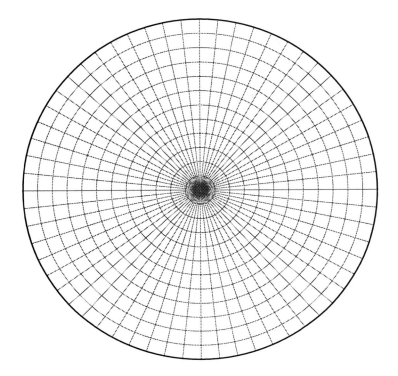

Now the main disadvantage of this variation is that, unlike all other key patterns, it does not use the diagonals, but follows the grid lines. This not only makes it look slightly different from the other keys, but gives it a tendency to revert to the classical S-curve shape ⌐⌐⌐. There are quite a few Celtic decorations like this, where the pattern is self-contained in each section, and rotated or reflected to fill the other sections, but this example will be based on the traditional key pattern shape.

So we divide the circle into equal sections, in this case 6 of them. The reason for choosing these dimensions is that the S-curve is generally roughly as wide as it is long. We will only draw the lines to 1 unit away from the outer circle and the centre of the circle. This is because these lines are to be the 'backbones' of the keys.

Then we draw the other 'backbones' down the middle of each space, again stopping 1 unit away from the outer circle and the centre of the circle. Then draw the next line, a curve, until it again is 1 unit away from the repeating section's edge. Then we draw the third lines, which stop 1 unit short of the centre of the section. This gives room for the opposite key line to be drawn in later. We carry on until the key is complete.

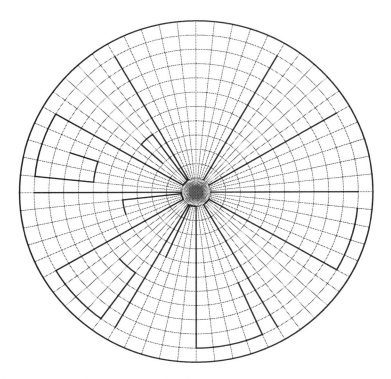

Then we do the same to the original dividing lines.

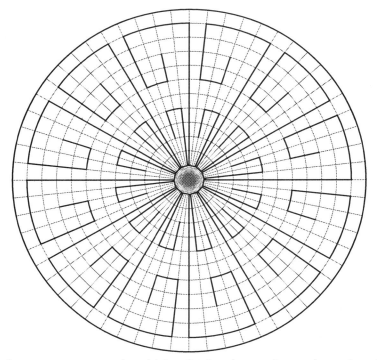

After all these key patterns, it should be fairly clear where the other keys have to go.

Although, as we can see, the classical S-curve manages to insinuate its way in even here.

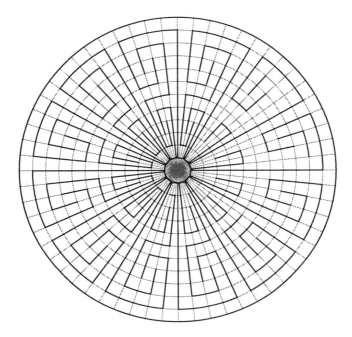

And there we have it. We can add weight to the pattern by 'flagging' the inner and outer edges, triangulating the ends or any of the other variations. Increasingly thickening the lines as you move further from the centre can be particularly effective.

A variation of this variation can be made by changing the grid. The concentric rings and 6

radial lines stay, but the other radial lines are drawn parallel to these 6 lines.

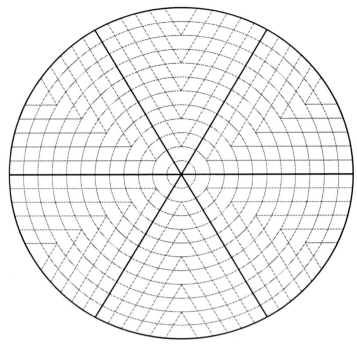

Then we just follow the same procedure as we did for the last variation, starting with the central line 'backbone'.

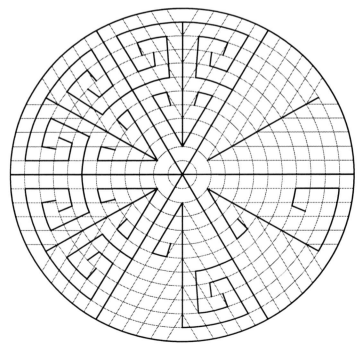

The result is a good-looking pattern, and one that is not too hard to create.

IRREGULAR KEY PATTERNS

Key patterns used to fill irregular areas are not that common, which may have something to do with the fact that their arrival coincided with the regular layout designs of the Christian period. There are examples and, as with the previous variation, there are two ways of drawing them. The grid can be drawn either by laying the key patterns out parallel to the nearest edge, so that all the points are roughly equidistant or they can be drawn so that they taper.

This time we will use the tapering grid to fill an area that is so extremely irregular that it would not normally be filled with a key pattern.

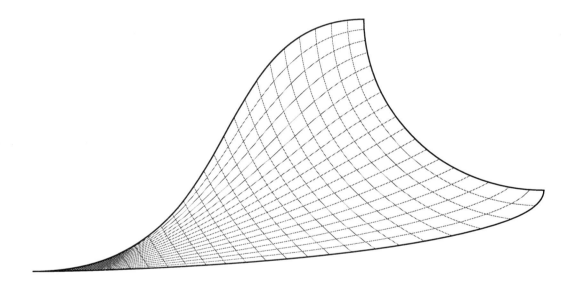

We have divided it into a 12 by 12 grid, so now we find a 12 by 12 rectangular pattern to fill it.

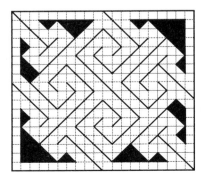

And now we just transpose the rectangular pattern onto the tapering grid, taking extreme care at the narrow end.

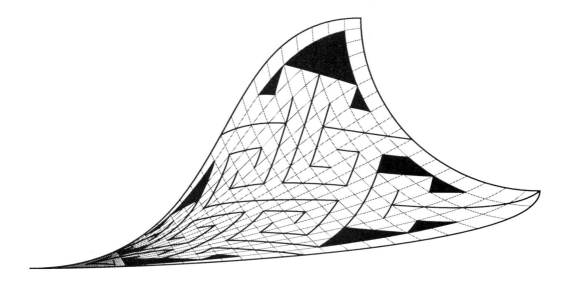

I have not seen any examples of keys drawn this way, but there is no reason for us not to do it, especially as it creates a rather striking pattern.

CURVED KEY PATTERNS

The last variation is a new, but rather obvious, one. As the keys are simply square S-curve spirals, why not go back to the basics and get rid of the square? All we have to do is take any key (in this case 1237) and make the square ends round.

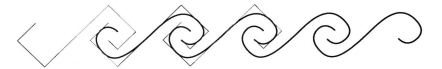

From here on it is just a case of transposing the curved keys onto the square pattern grid.

Working out what the edge triangles become is a bit harder but, with judicious use of the '1 unit away' rule and a bit of averaging and smoothing, we have it.

The final result looks very different from the rigid keys in the rest of this book, and it is very strange that the Celts of the sixth and seventh centuries did not apply their talents to this, a pattern which is like the traditional Celtic style of old, and rather less like the style of the golden age of Christian Celtic art. Their loss is our gain, as it gives us a chance to further explore designs that no one has seen before.

THE SECTIONS

The following pages show each of the nine sections needed to make each of the seven most basic key patterns. The nine sections are preceded by a full-page image using that pattern on its own, then followed by the four inside corners which are used for drawing boxes within the key patterns.

The complete pattern image shows the smallest version of the pattern with that page's section highlighted. This is mainly to let you skim through this chapter and choose the pattern you want.

The outline section shows both the thin and thick line versions. Each section is marked with the appropriate grid lines, the size of which is given under the section name. This is particularly useful for creating larger stencils for decorating or printing, or for scaling down to create smaller patterns.

The other measurements given are for the charted patterns. First the size is given (in units) for the central repeat section, and below that the sizes of the minimum key square (see page 66) and the smallest complete pattern (as shown at the top of each page). To calculate the size for a larger pattern simply add the numbers for the minimum key square to as many multiples of the numbers of the central repeat section size as you want. I have tried to give as wide a variety of repeat sizes with the different keys as possible, so that most rectangular areas can be filled.

At the bottom of each page are two charted patterns for each section. On the left is the thin line version and on the right the thick line version. Unlike *How to Draw Celtic Knotwork*, there are no charted sections for the 'Pictish' proportions of 4 by 3. This is because the diagonal lines that are the heart of key patterns do not translate well onto charted grids of this scale, and the regularity of the pattern, if not the entire thing, is lost.

All of these sections should prove useful to start you off, and can be adapted by making any of the variations shown in this book (and any others that you can think of), but you should soon be able to start to work out new patterns. As with most things, the more you practise the easier it gets. Above all, enjoy.

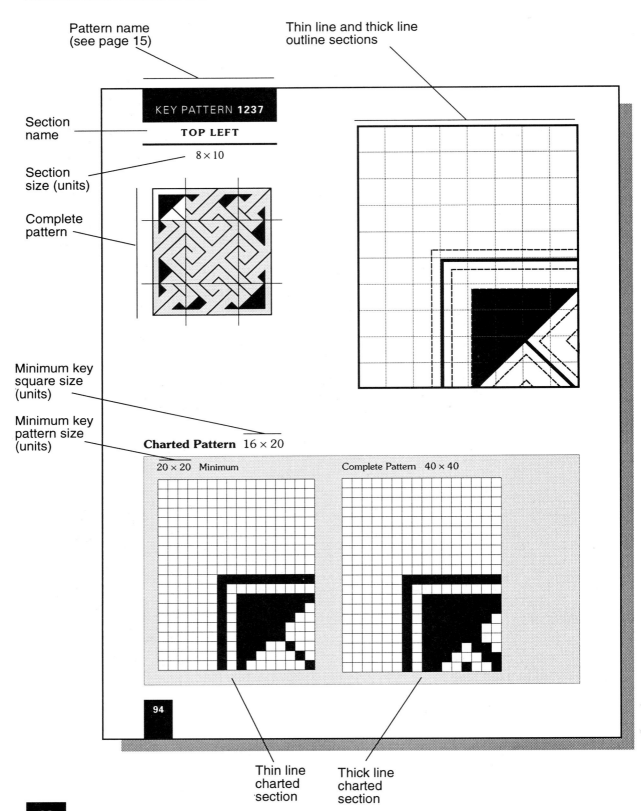

Pattern name
(see page 15)

Thin line and thick line
outline sections

KEY PATTERN **1237**

TOP LEFT

8×10

Section
name

Section
size (units)

Complete
pattern

Minimum key
square size
(units)

Minimum key
pattern size
(units)

Charted Pattern 16×20

20×20 Minimum

Complete Pattern 40×40

94

Thin line
charted
section

Thick line
charted
section

TOP LEFT

8×10

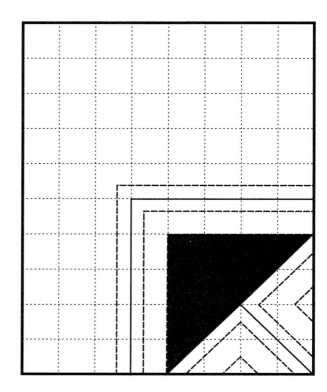

Charted Pattern 16×20

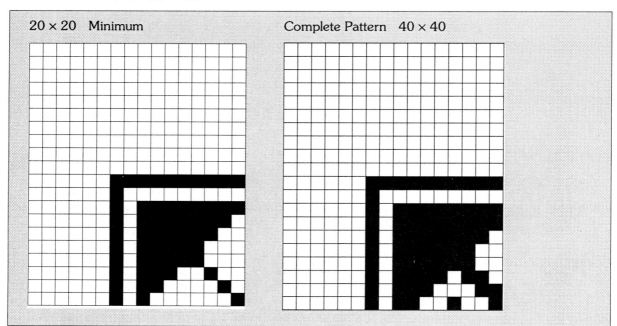

20×20 Minimum

Complete Pattern 40×40

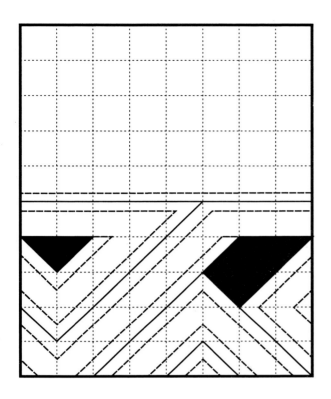

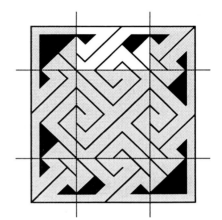

Charted Pattern 16×20

20×20 Minimum

Complete Pattern 40×40

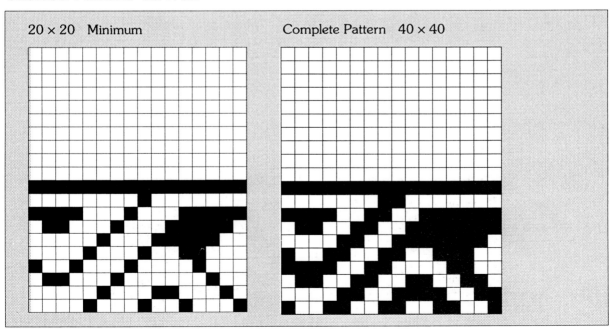

TOP RIGHT

8 × 10

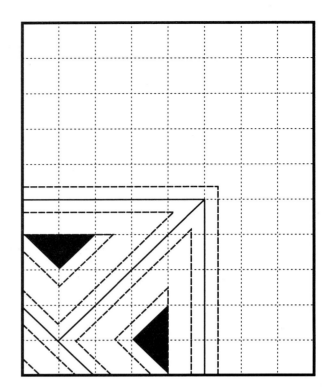

Charted Pattern   16 × 20

20 × 20 Minimum

Complete Pattern 40 × 40

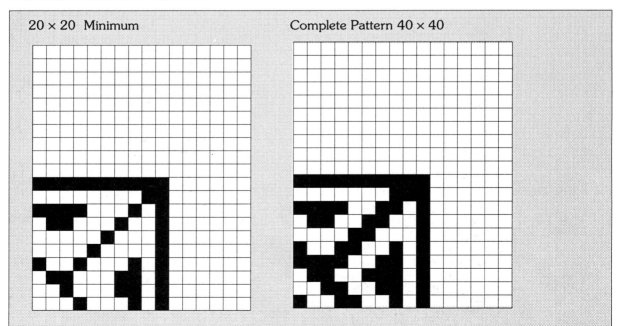

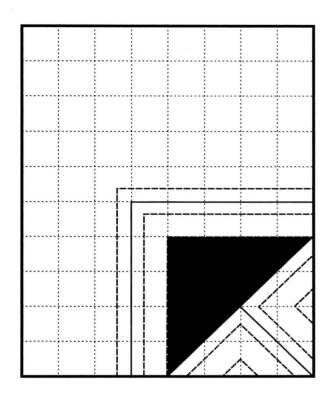

MIDDLE LEFT

8×10

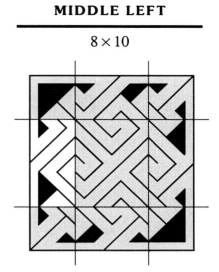

Charted Pattern 16×20

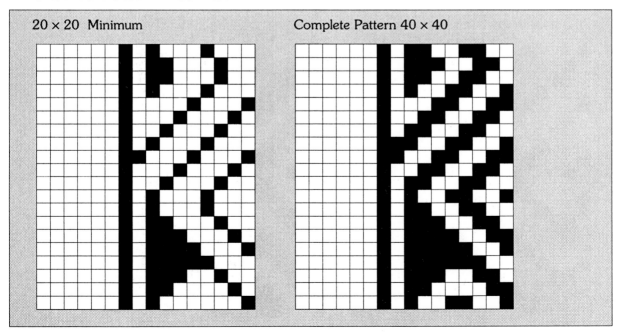

20 × 20 Minimum

Complete Pattern 40 × 40

MIDDLE CENTRE

8 × 10

Charted Pattern   16 × 20

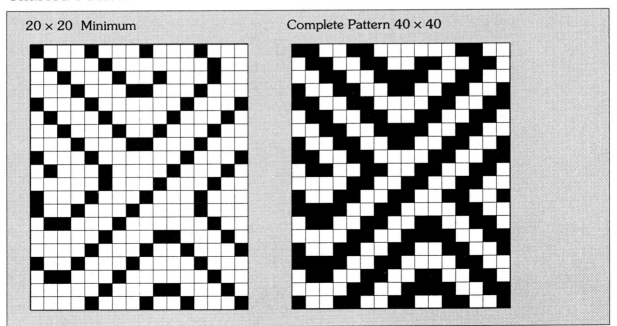

20 × 20 Minimum

Complete Pattern 40 × 40

MIDDLE RIGHT

8×10

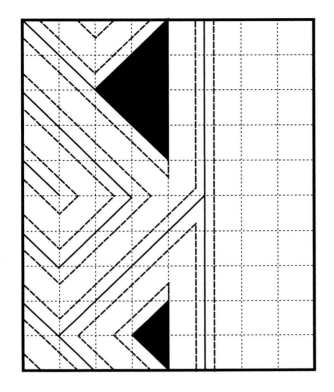

Charted Pattern 16×20

20 × 20 Minimum   Complete Pattern 40 × 40

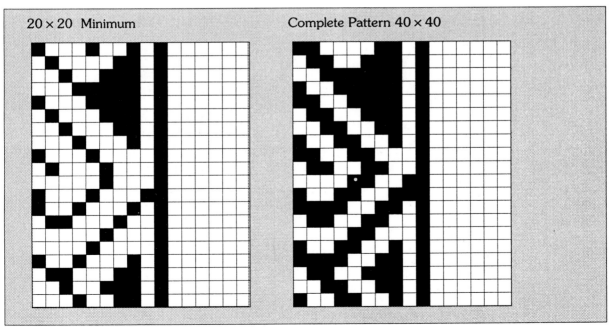

BOTTOM LEFT

8×10

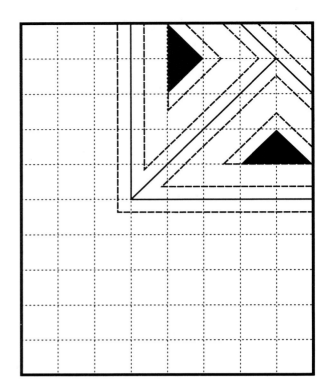

Charted Pattern 16×20

20 × 20 Minimum

Complete Pattern 40 × 40

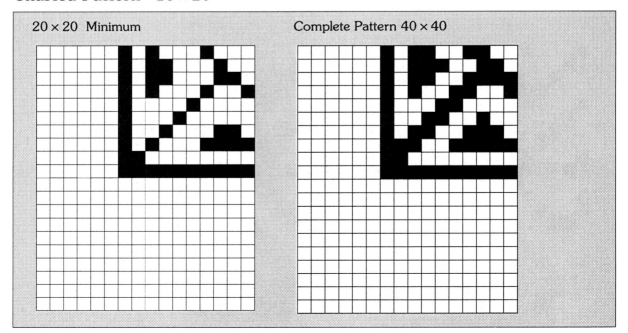

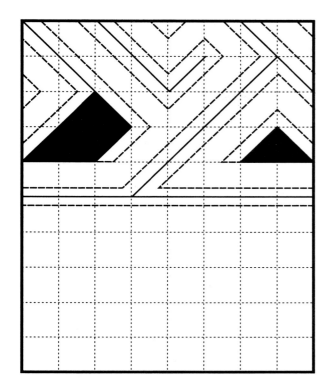

BOTTOM CENTRE

8×10

Charted Pattern 16×20

20×20 Minimum

Complete Pattern 40×40

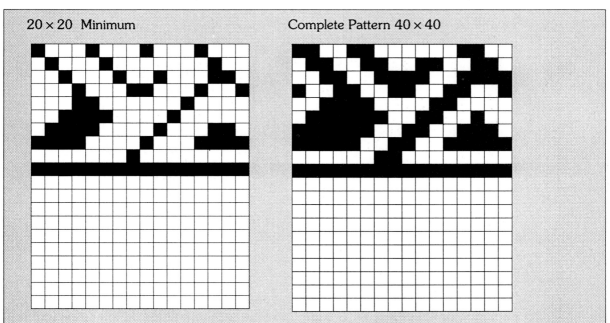

BOTTOM RIGHT

8×10

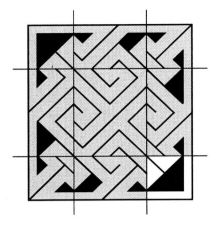

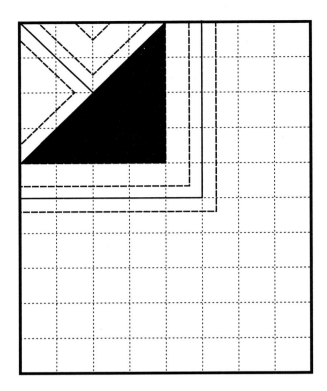

Charted Pattern 16×20

20 × 20 Minimum   Complete Pattern 40 × 40

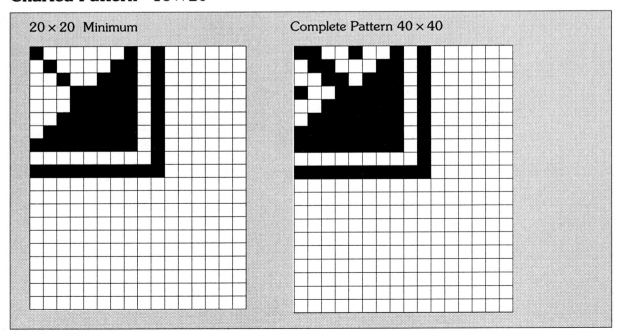

INNER TOP LEFT

8×10

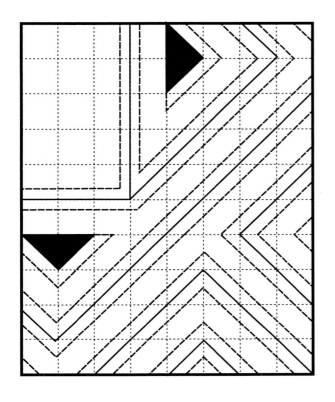

Charted Pattern 16×20

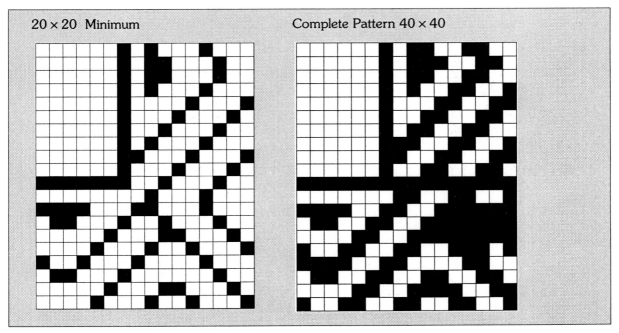

20 × 20 Minimum

Complete Pattern 40 × 40

INNER TOP RIGHT

8×10

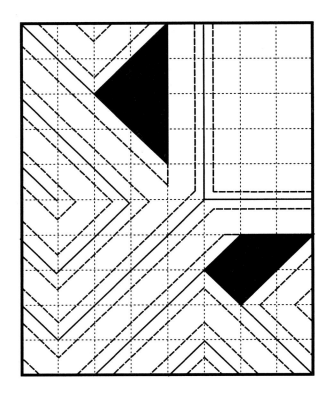

Charted Pattern 16×20

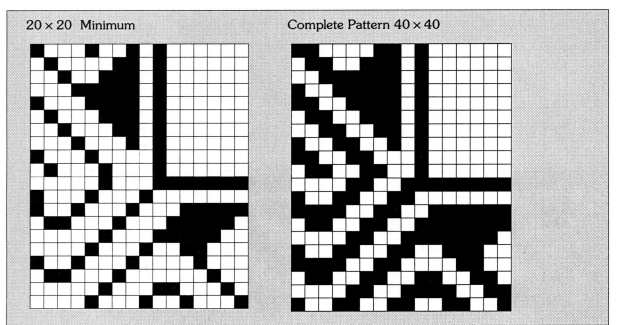

20 × 20 Minimum

Complete Pattern 40 × 40

INNER BOTTOM LEFT

8×10

Charted Pattern 16×20

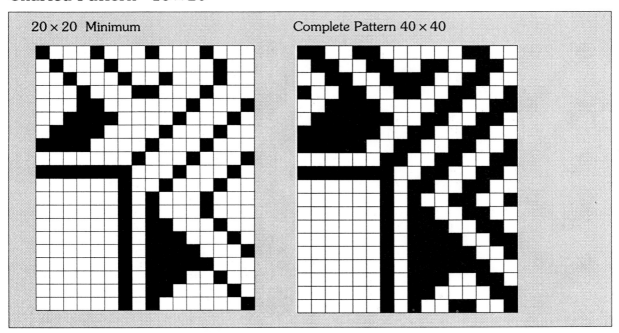

20×20 Minimum

Complete Pattern 40×40

INNER BOTTOM RIGHT

8 × 10

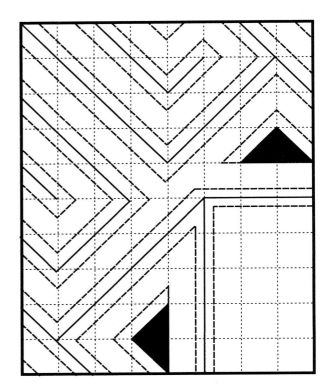

Charted Pattern   16 × 20

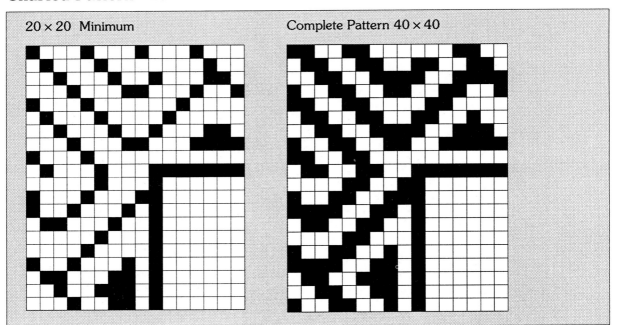

20 × 20 Minimum

Complete Pattern 40 × 40

KEY PATTERN **1237Y**

TOP LEFT

8×10

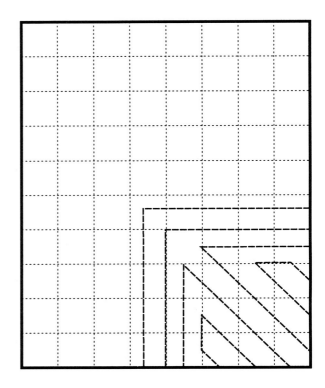

Charted Pattern 16×20

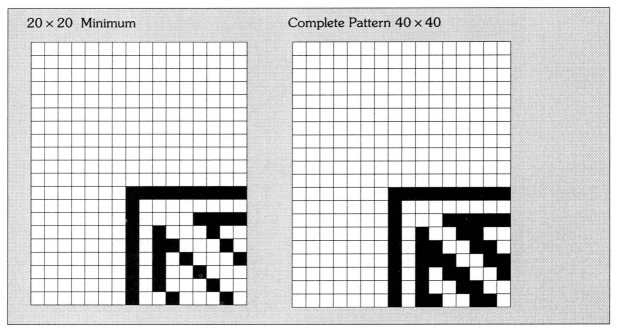

20×20 Minimum

Complete Pattern 40×40

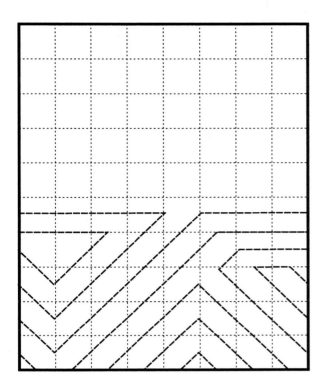

TOP CENTRE

8×10

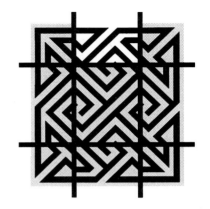

Charted Pattern 16×20

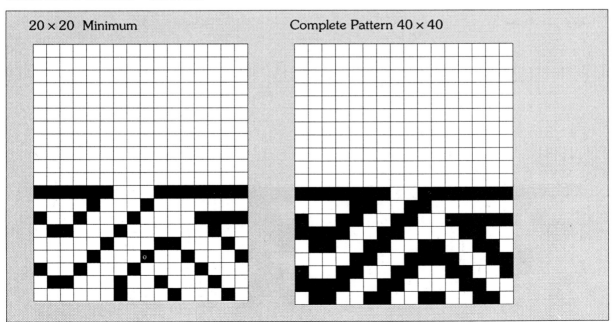

20 × 20 Minimum

Complete Pattern 40 × 40

TOP RIGHT

8×10

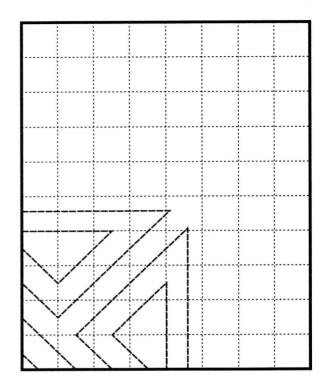

Charted Pattern 16×20

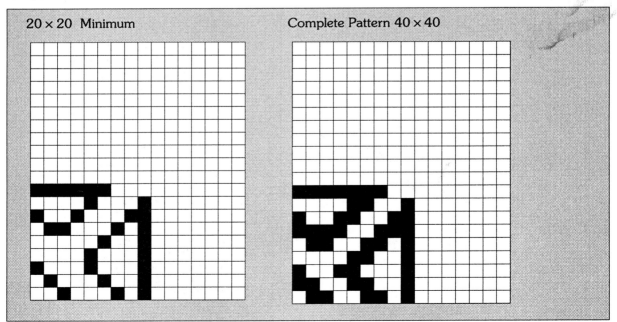

20 × 20 Minimum

Complete Pattern 40 × 40

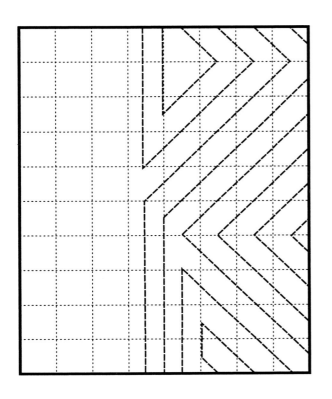

Charted Pattern 16×20

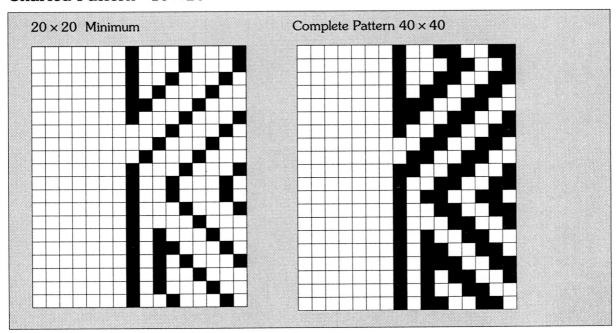

20 × 20 Minimum

Complete Pattern 40 × 40

MIDDLE CENTRE

8×10

Charted Pattern 16×20

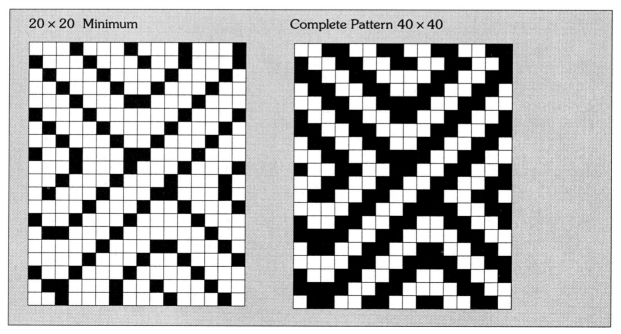

20×20 Minimum

Complete Pattern 40×40

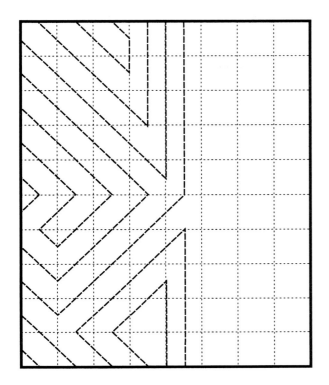

Charted Pattern 16×20

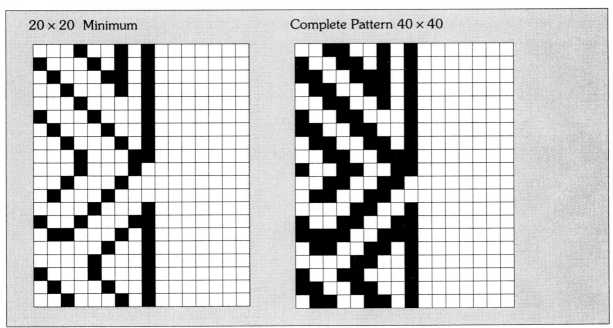

20 × 20 Minimum

Complete Pattern 40 × 40

BOTTOM LEFT

8×10

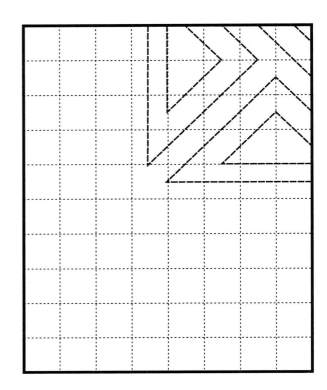

Charted Pattern 16×20

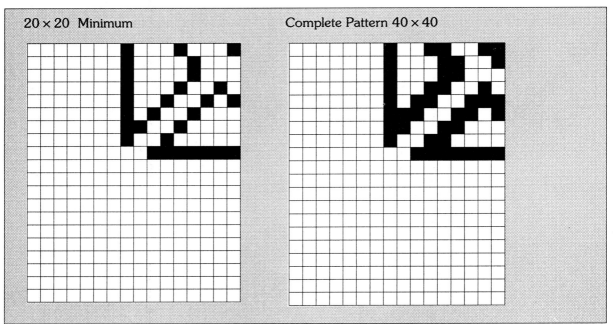

20×20 Minimum

Complete Pattern 40×40

8×10

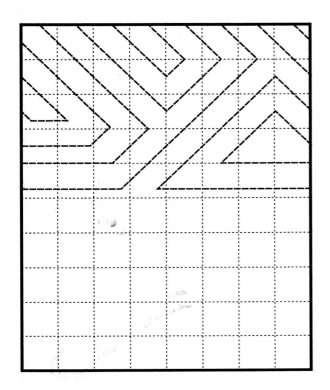

Charted Pattern 16×20

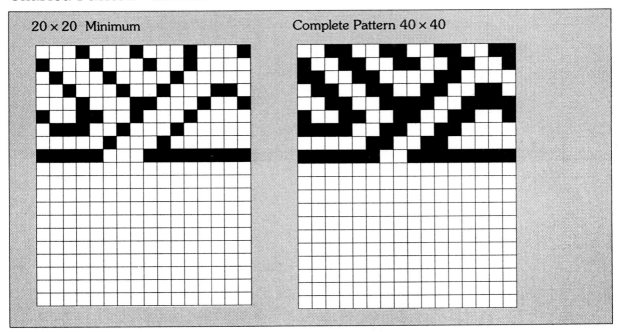

20 × 20 Minimum

Complete Pattern 40 × 40

BOTTOM RIGHT

8 × 10

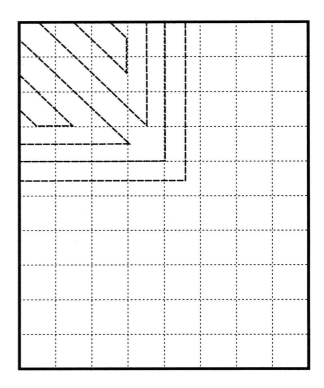

Charted Pattern 16 × 20

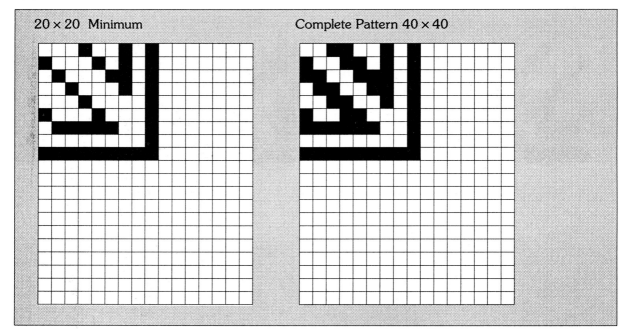

20 × 20 Minimum

Complete Pattern 40 × 40

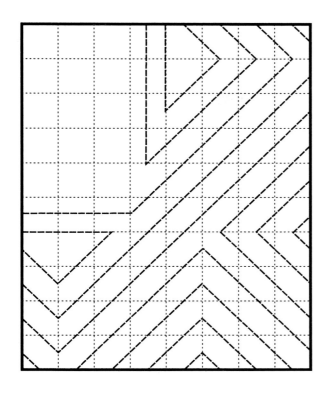

Charted Pattern 16×20

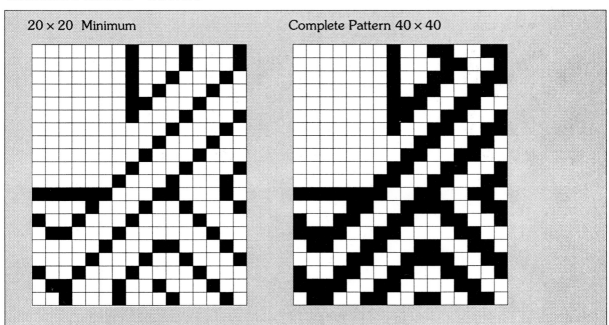

20×20 Minimum

Complete Pattern 40×40

INNER TOP RIGHT

8 × 10

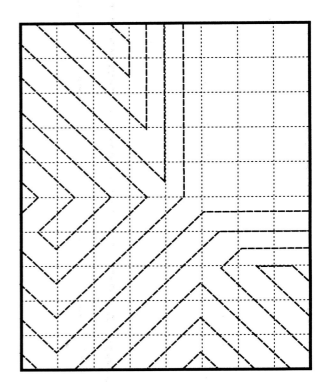

Charted Pattern 16 × 20

20 × 20 Minimum   Complete Pattern 40 × 40

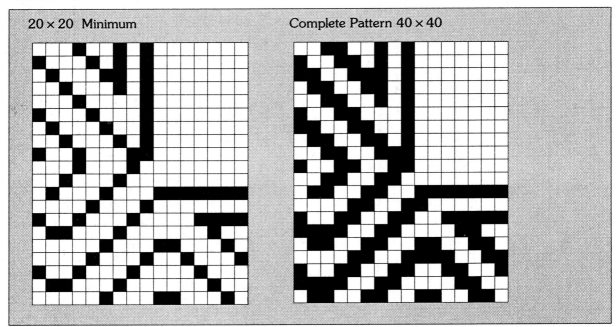

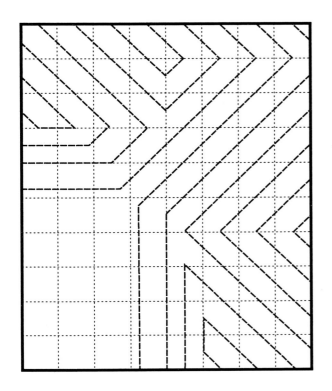

INNER BOTTOM LEFT

8×10

Charted Pattern 16×20

20 × 20 Minimum

Complete Pattern 40 × 40

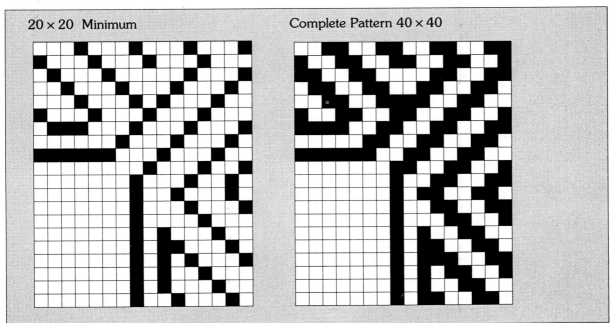

INNER BOTTOM RIGHT

8 × 10

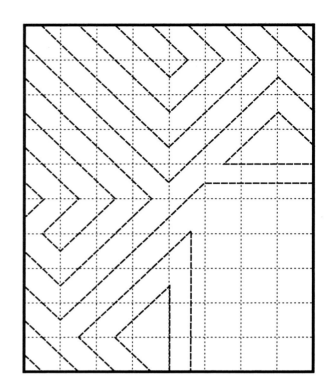

Charted Pattern   16 × 20

20 × 20 Minimum   Complete Pattern 40 × 40

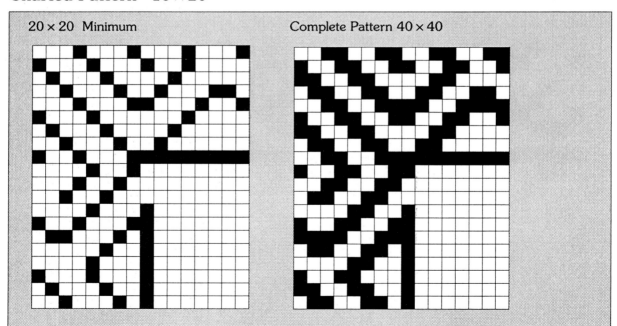

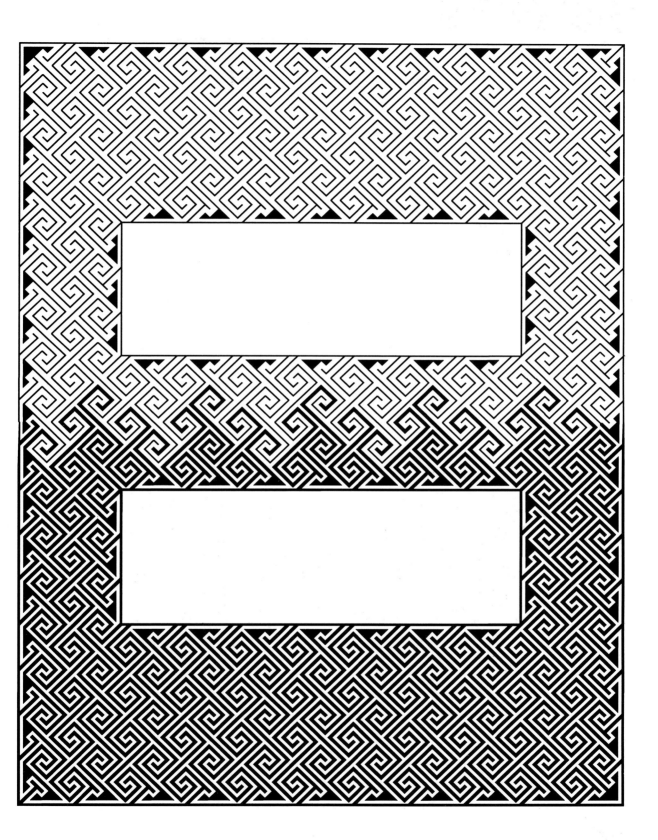

TOP LEFT

12×10

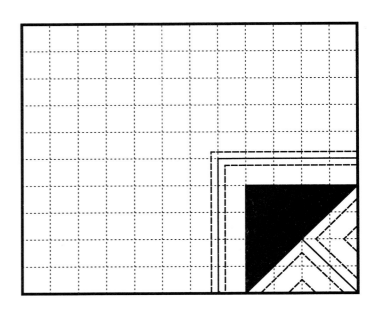

Charted Pattern 24×20

22 × 22 Minimum   Complete Pattern 46 × 42

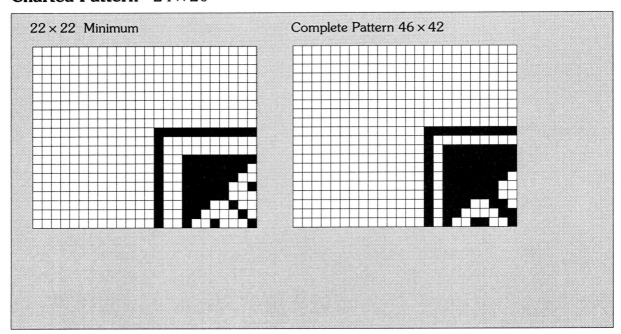

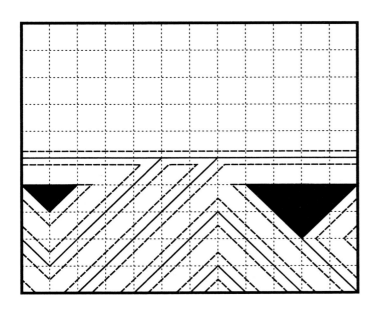

TOP CENTRE

12×10

Charted Pattern 24×20

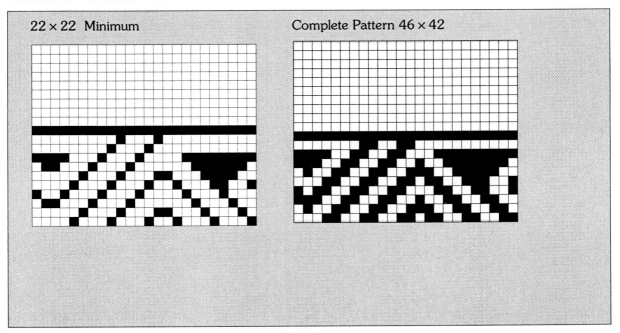

22×22 Minimum

Complete Pattern 46×42

TOP RIGHT

12×10

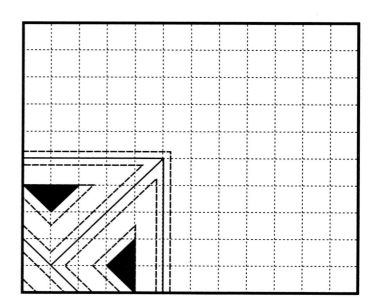

Charted Pattern 24×20

22 × 22 Minimum

Complete Pattern 46 × 42

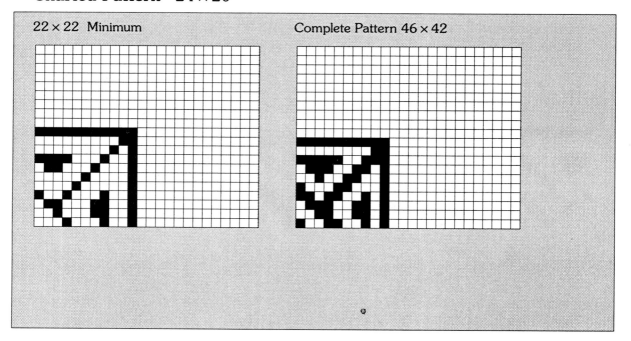

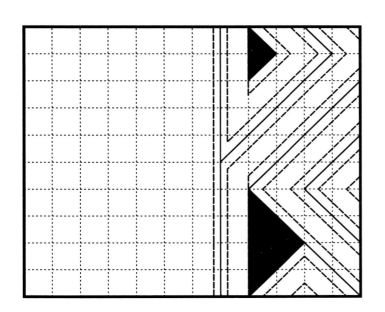

Charted Pattern 24×20

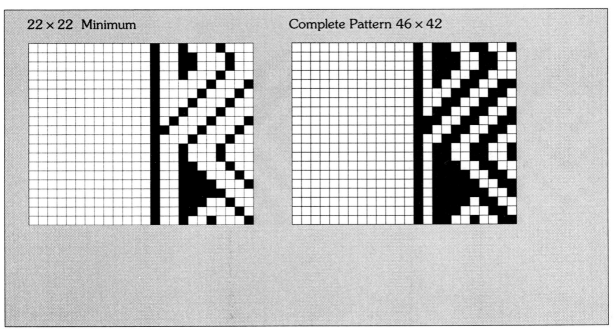

22 × 22 Minimum

Complete Pattern 46 × 42

MIDDLE CENTRE

12 × 10

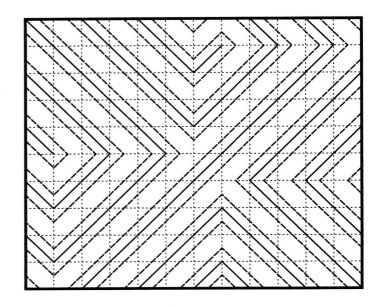

Charted Pattern 24 × 20

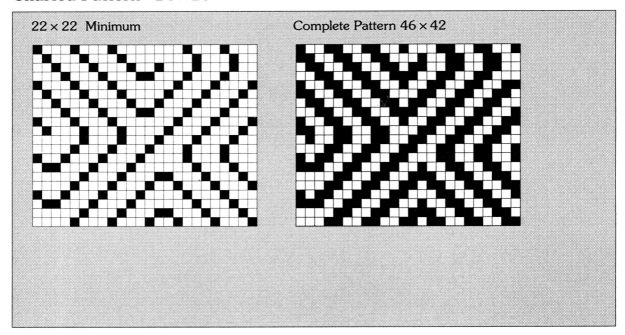

22 × 22 Minimum

Complete Pattern 46 × 42

MIDDLE RIGHT

12×10

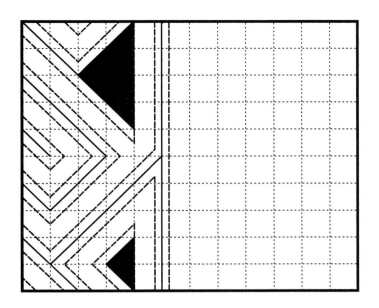

Charted Pattern 24×20

22 × 22 Minimum

Complete Pattern 46 × 42

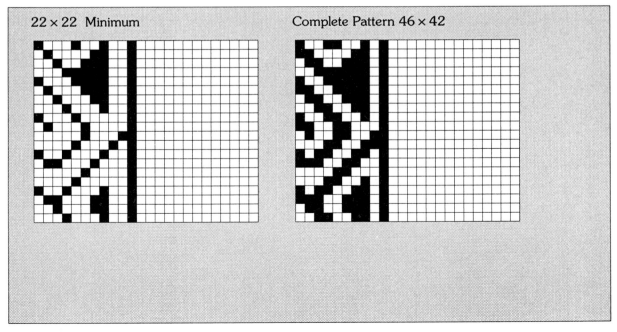

BOTTOM LEFT

12×10

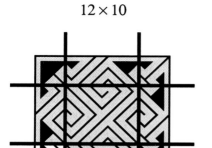

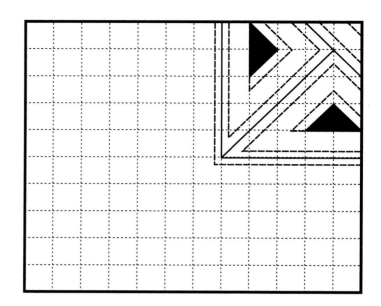

Charted Pattern 24×20

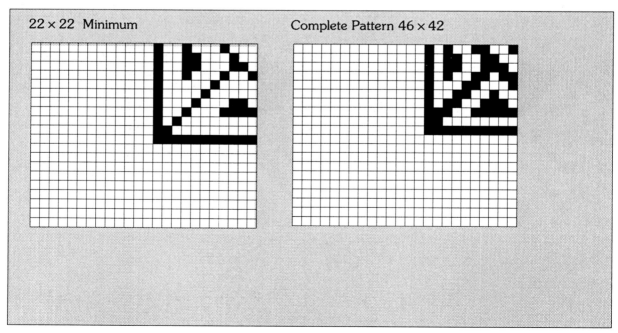

22×22 Minimum

Complete Pattern 46×42

BOTTOM CENTRE

12×10

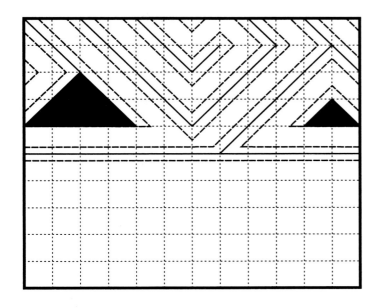

Charted Pattern 24×20

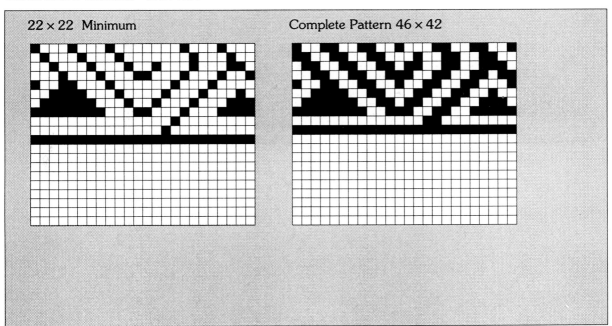

22 × 22 Minimum

Complete Pattern 46 × 42

BOTTOM RIGHT

12 × 10

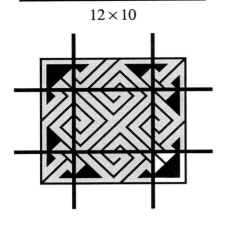

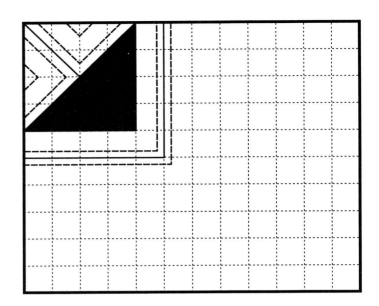

Charted Pattern   24 × 20

22 × 22 Minimum   Complete Pattern 46 × 42

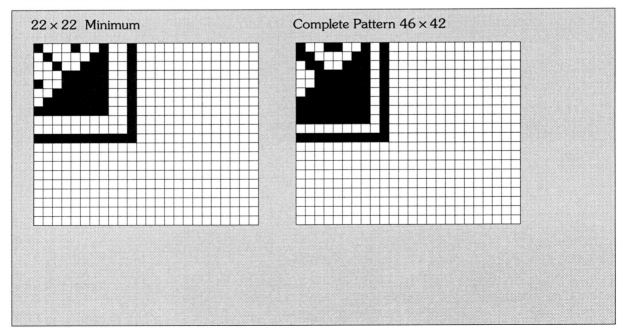

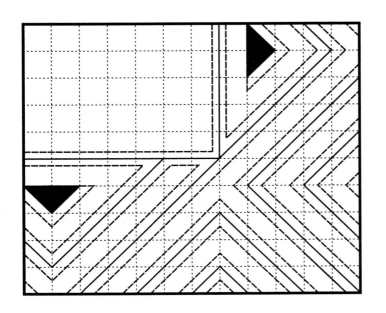

Charted Pattern 24×20

22×22 Minimum

Complete Pattern 46×42

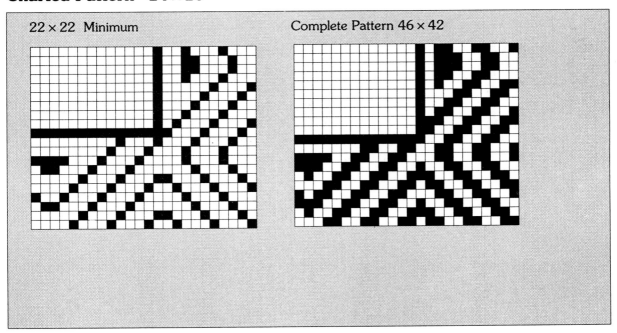

INNER TOP RIGHT

12×10

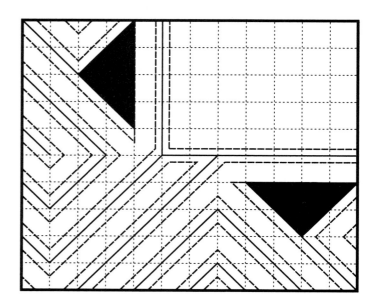

Charted Pattern 24×20

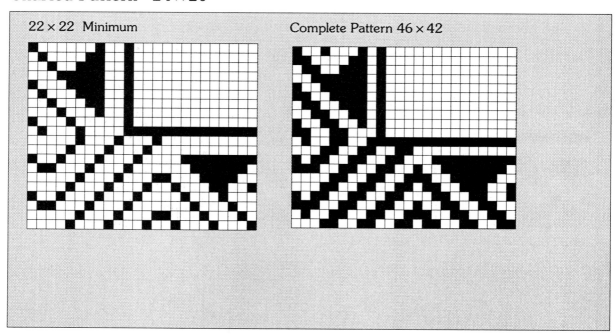

22×22 Minimum

Complete Pattern 46×42

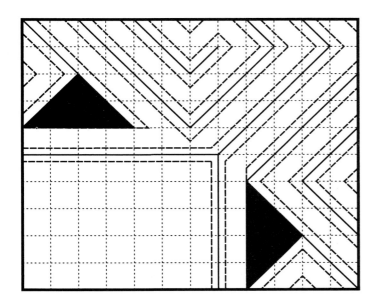

INNER BOTTOM LEFT

12×10

Charted Pattern 24×20

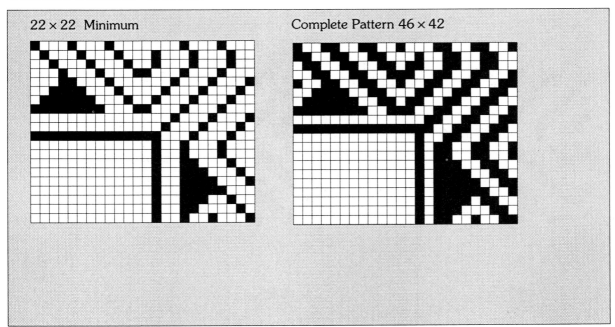

22×22 Minimum

Complete Pattern 46×42

INNER BOTTOM RIGHT

12×10

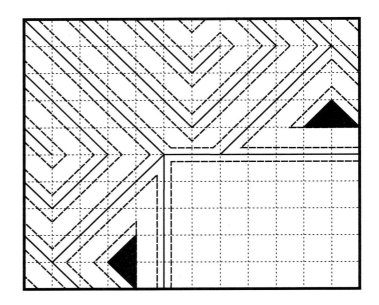

Charted Pattern 24×20

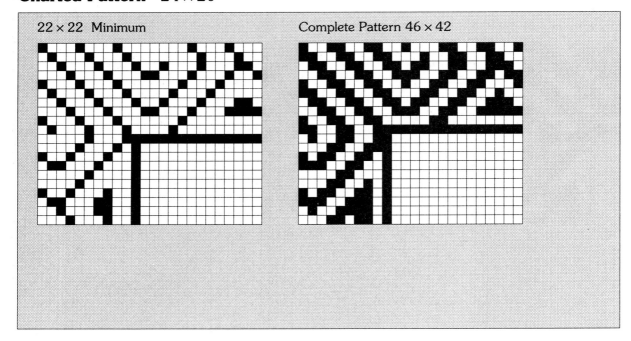

22 × 22 Minimum   Complete Pattern 46 × 42

TOP LEFT

12×10

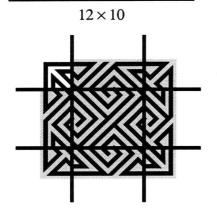

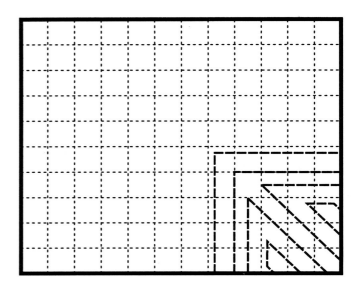

Charted Pattern 24×20

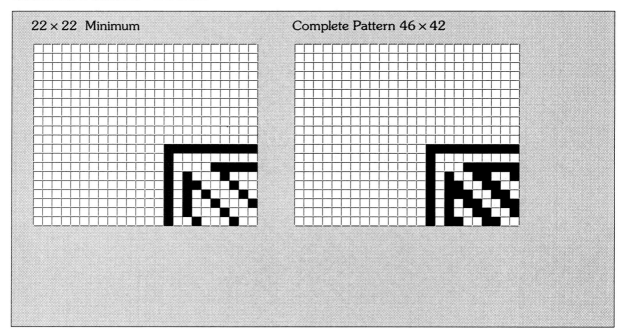

22×22 Minimum

Complete Pattern 46×42

12×10

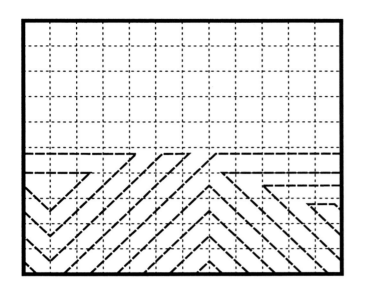

Charted Pattern 24×20

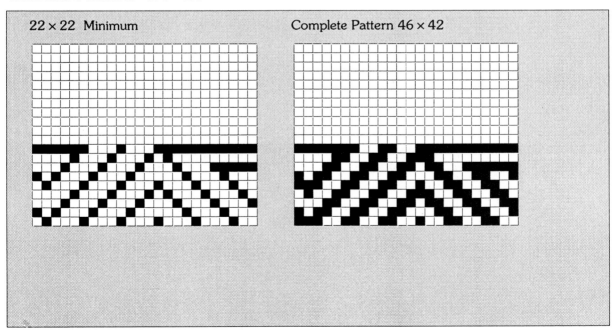

22×22 Minimum

Complete Pattern 46×42

TOP RIGHT

12 × 10

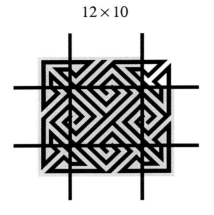

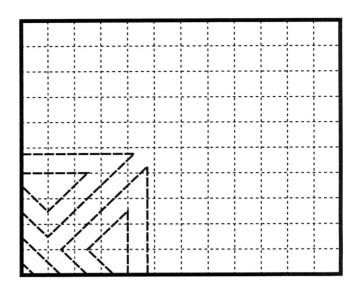

Charted Pattern 24 × 20

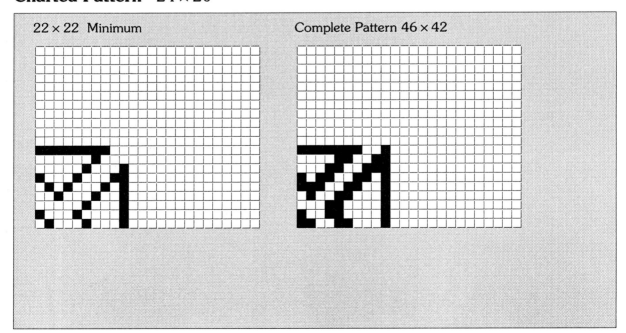

22 × 22 Minimum

Complete Pattern 46 × 42

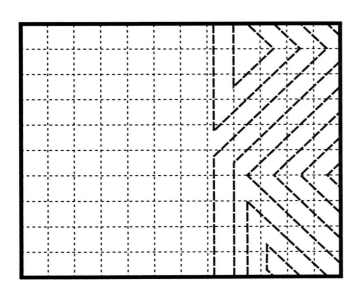

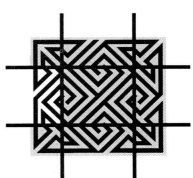
Charted Pattern 24×20

22 × 22 Minimum

Complete Pattern 46 × 42

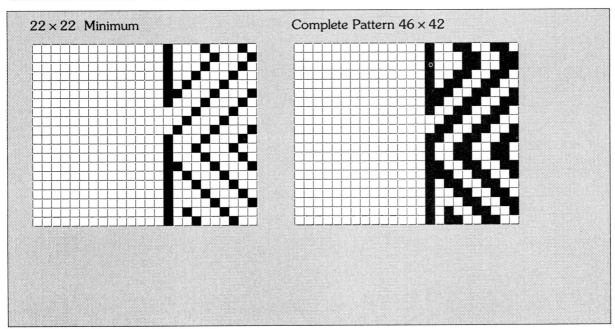

MIDDLE CENTRE

12 × 10

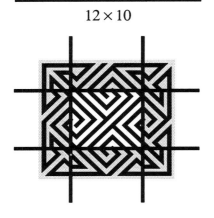

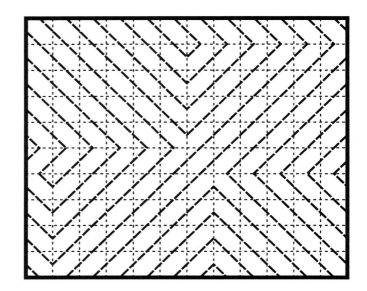

Charted Pattern 24 × 20

22 × 22 Minimum

Complete Pattern 46 × 42

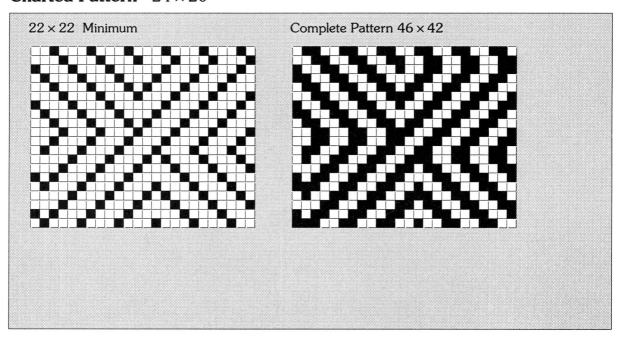

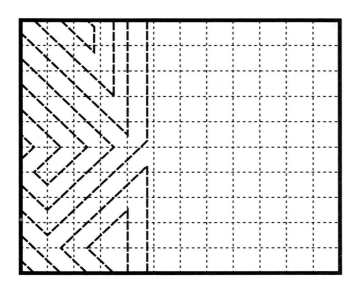

12×10

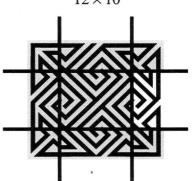

Charted Pattern 24×20

22×22 Minimum

Complete Pattern 46×42

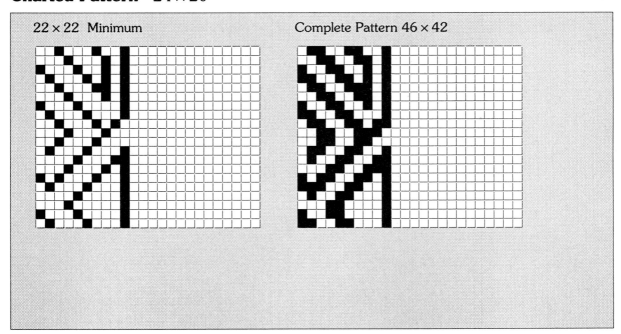

BOTTOM LEFT

12×10

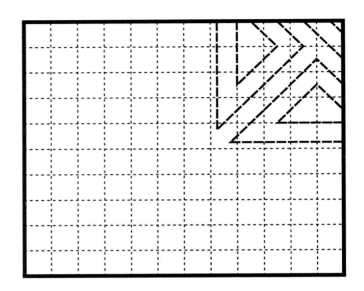

Charted Pattern 24×20

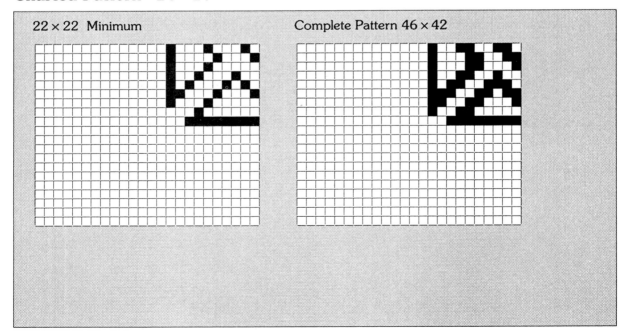

22×22 Minimum

Complete Pattern 46×42

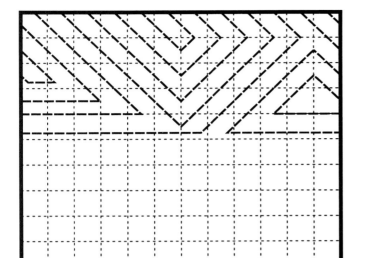

BOTTOM CENTRE

12×10

Charted Pattern 24×20

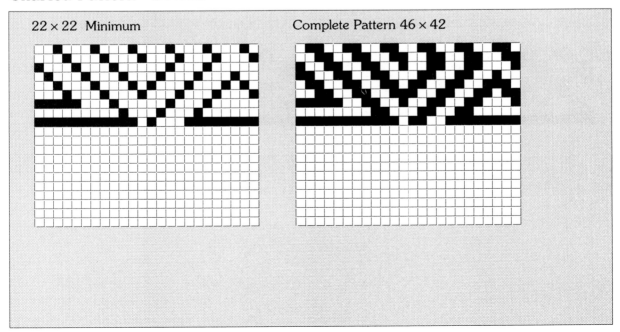

22×22 Minimum

Complete Pattern 46×42

BOTTOM RIGHT

12×10

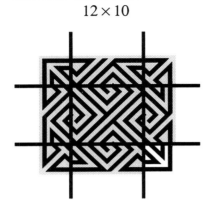

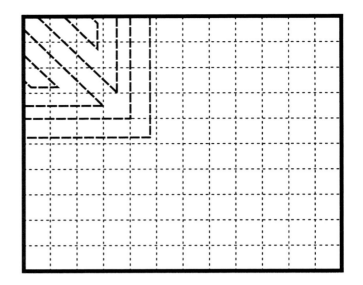

Charted Pattern 24×20

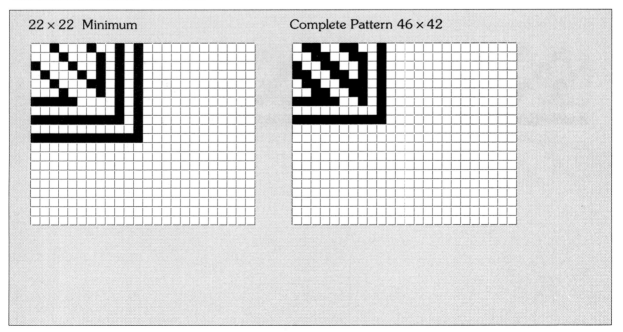

22 × 22 Minimum

Complete Pattern 46 × 42

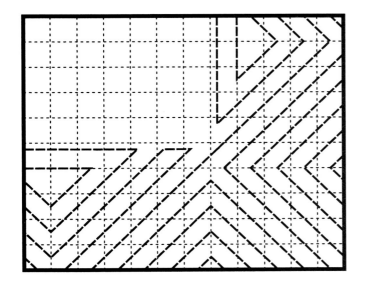

INNER TOP LEFT

12×10

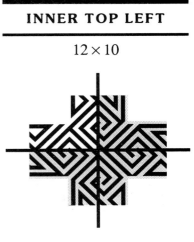

Charted Pattern 24×20

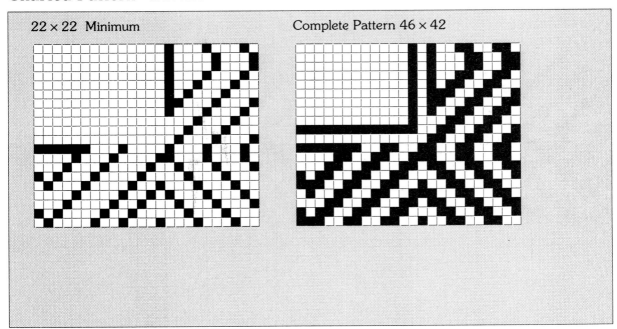

22×22 Minimum

Complete Pattern 46×42

INNER TOP RIGHT

12×10

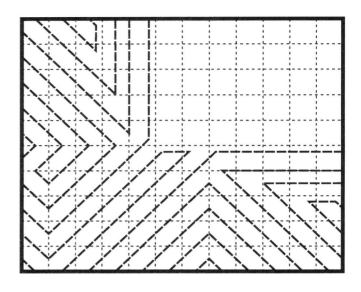

Charted Pattern 24×20

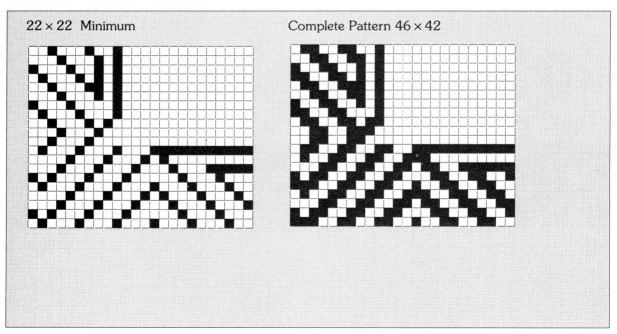

22 × 22 Minimum

Complete Pattern 46 × 42

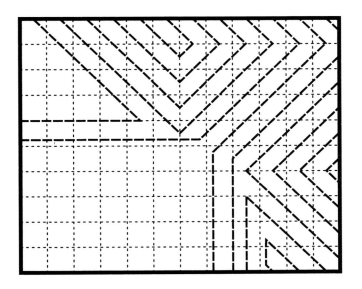

Charted Pattern 24×20

22×22 Minimum

Complete Pattern 46×42

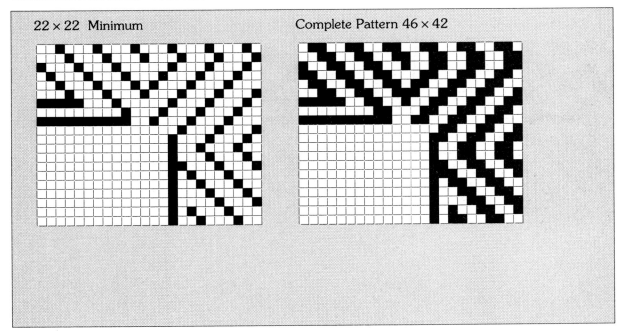

INNER BOTTOM RIGHT

12 × 10

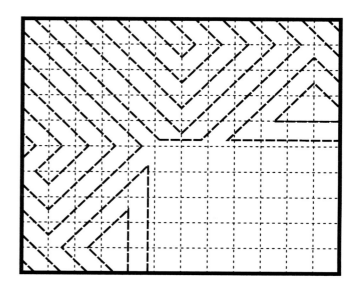

Charted Pattern   24 × 20

22 × 22 Minimum

Complete Pattern 46 × 42

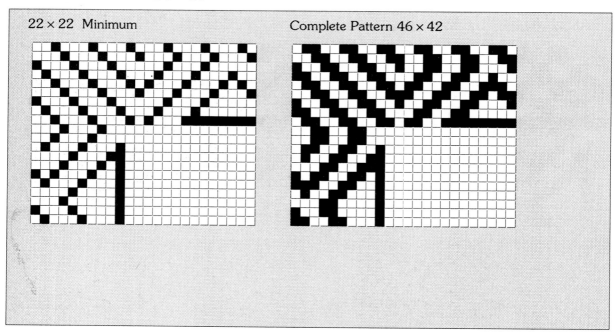

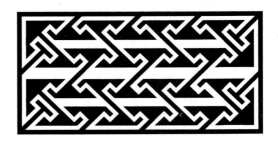

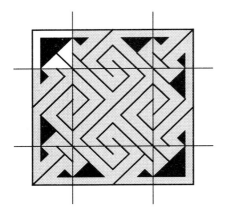

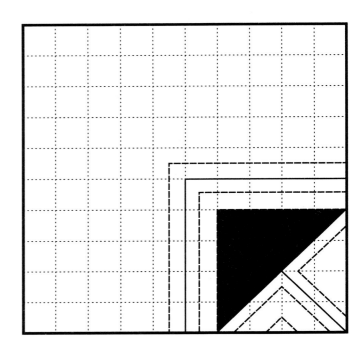

Charted Pattern 20×20

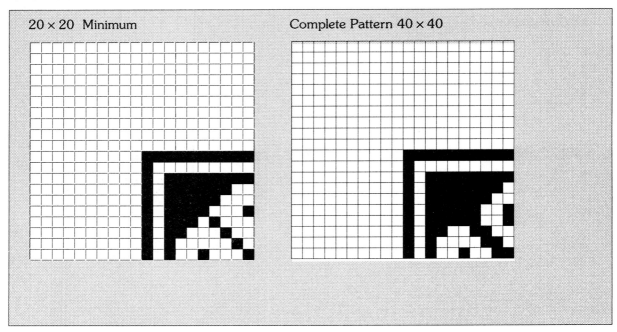

20×20 Minimum

Complete Pattern 40×40

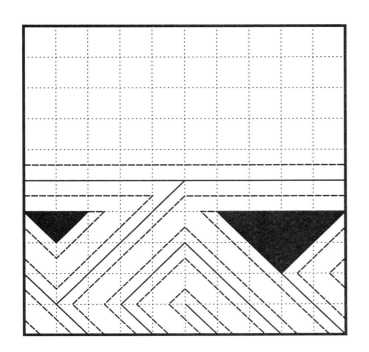

TOP CENTRE

10×10

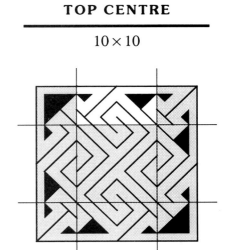

Charted Pattern 20×20

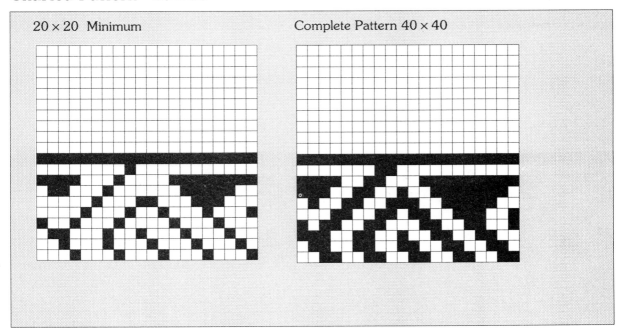

20 × 20 Minimum

Complete Pattern 40 × 40

TOP RIGHT

10 × 10

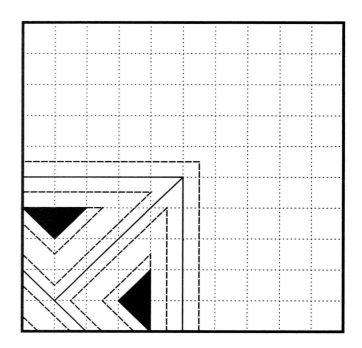

Charted Pattern   20 × 20

20 × 20 Minimum

Complete Pattern 40 × 40

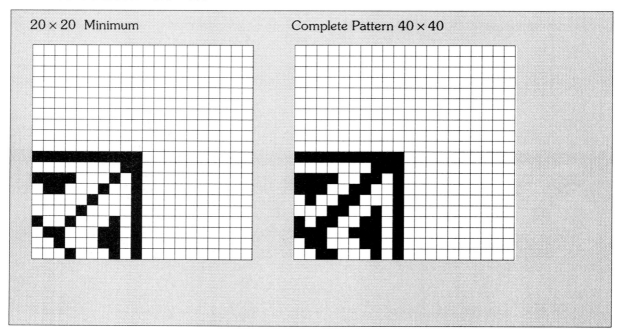

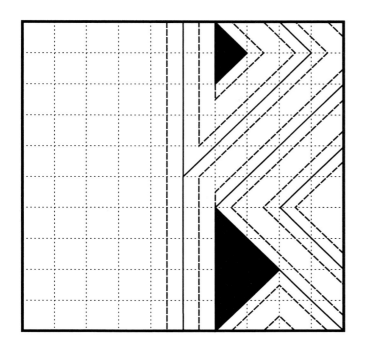

MIDDLE LEFT

10×10

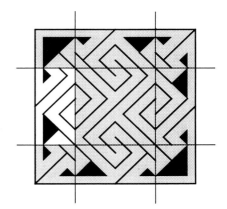

Charted Pattern 20×20

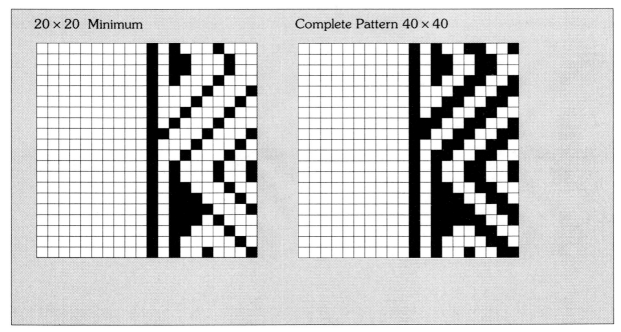

20 × 20 Minimum

Complete Pattern 40 × 40

MIDDLE CENTRE

10×10

Charted Pattern 20×20

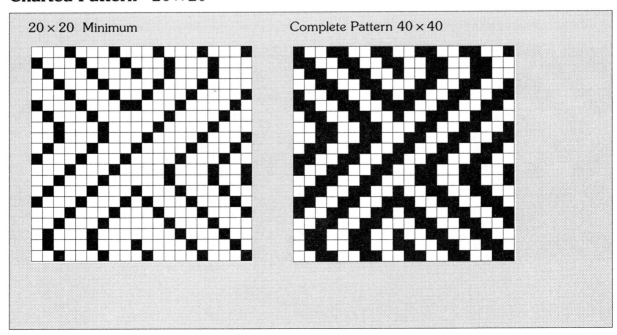

20×20 Minimum

Complete Pattern 40×40

MIDDLE RIGHT

10×10

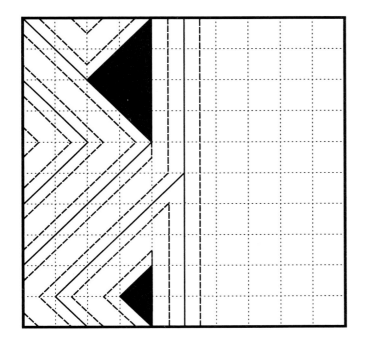

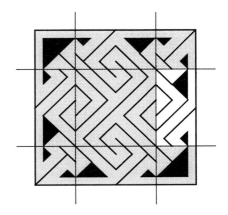

Charted Pattern 20×20

20×20 Minimum

Complete Pattern 40×40

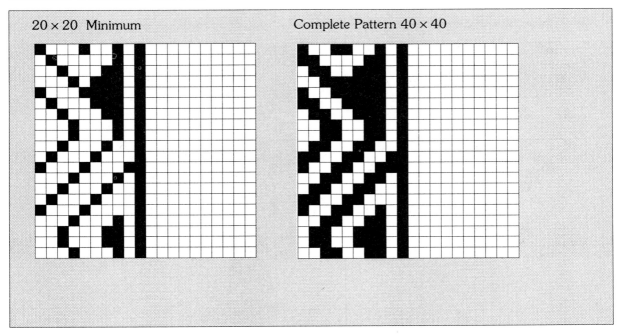

BOTTOM LEFT

10×10

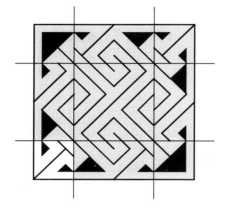

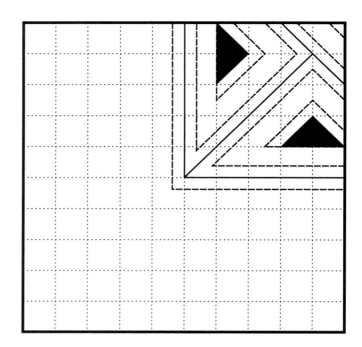

Charted Pattern 20×20

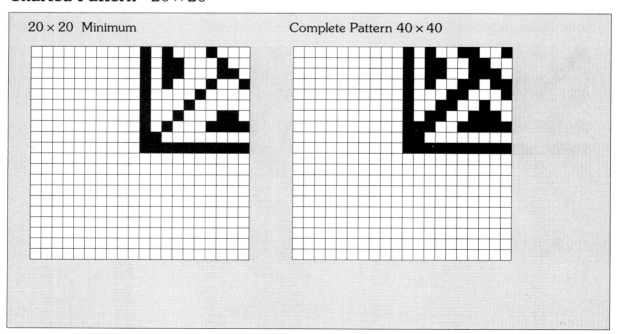

20×20 Minimum

Complete Pattern 40×40

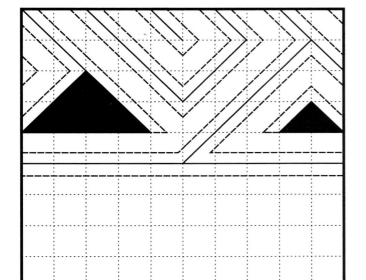

BOTTOM CENTRE

10×10

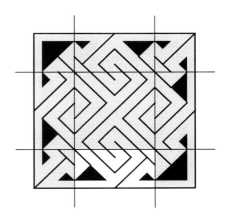

Charted Pattern 20×20

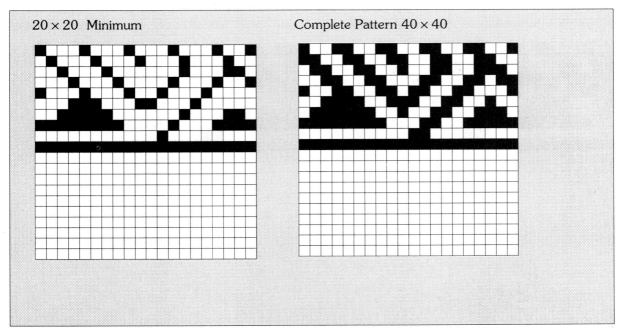

20×20 Minimum

Complete Pattern 40×40

BOTTOM RIGHT

10×10

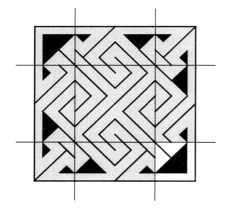

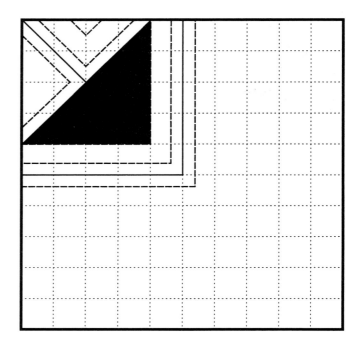

Charted Pattern 20×20

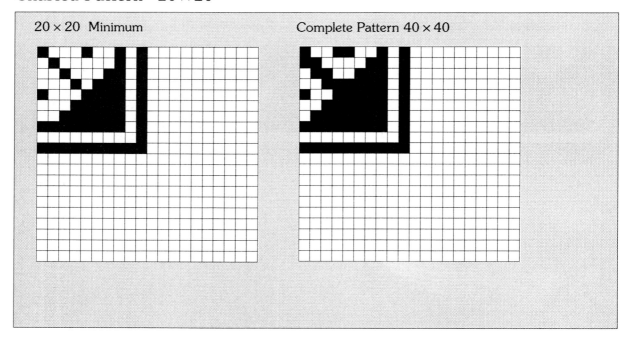

20×20 Minimum

Complete Pattern 40×40

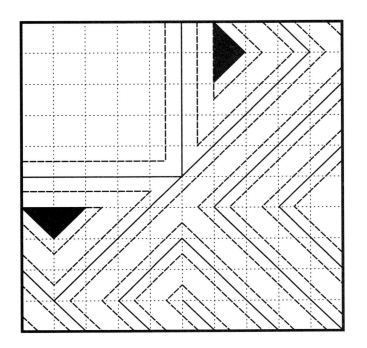

INNER TOP LEFT

10×10

Charted Pattern 20×20

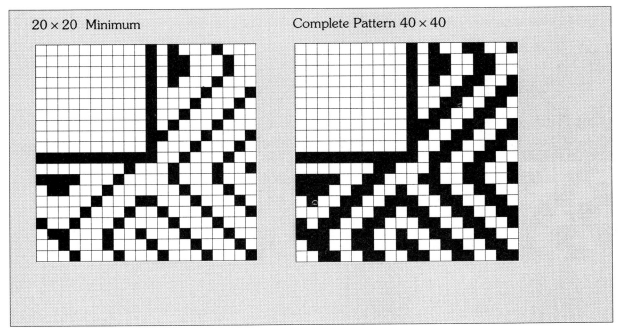

20×20 Minimum

Complete Pattern 40×40

10×10

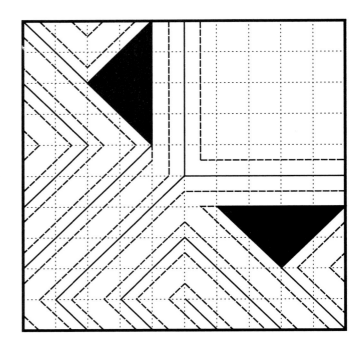

Charted Pattern 20×20

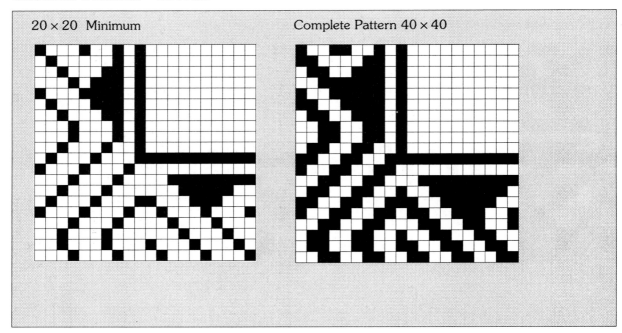

20×20 Minimum

Complete Pattern 40×40

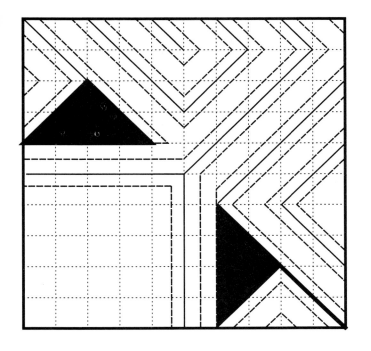

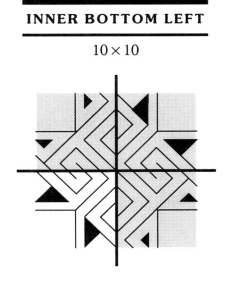

Charted Pattern 20×20

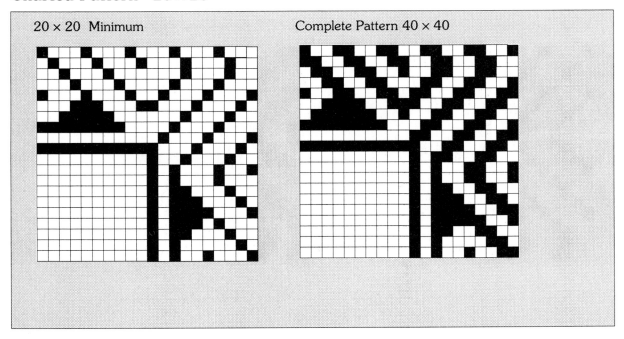

20×20 Minimum   Complete Pattern 40×40

INNER BOTTOM RIGHT

10×10

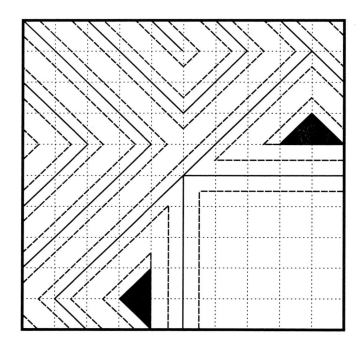

Charted Pattern 20×20

20×20 Minimum

Complete Pattern 40×40

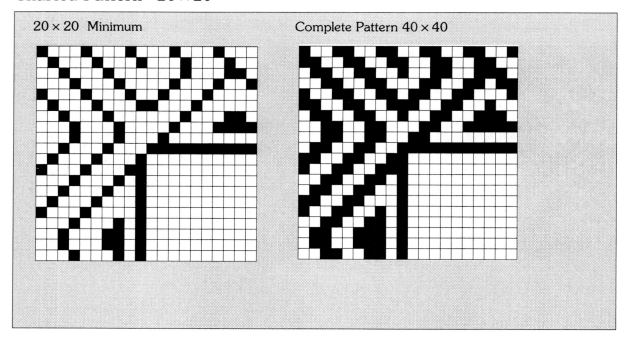

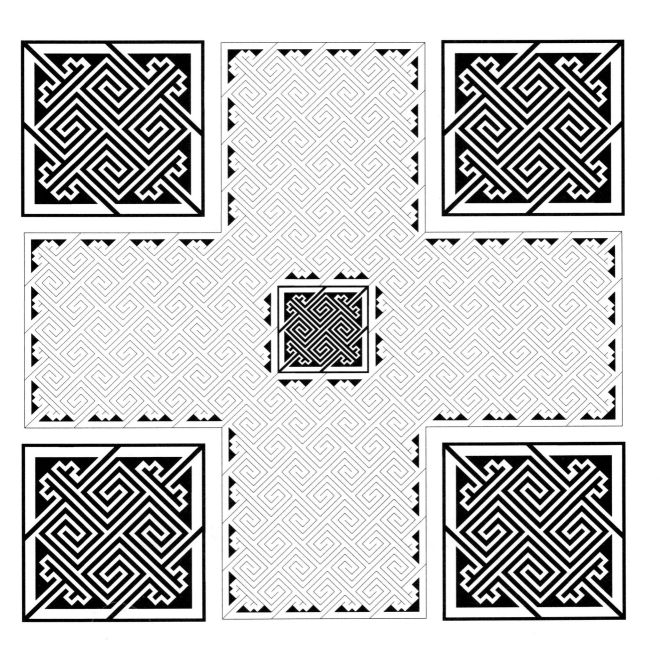

TOP LEFT

14×14

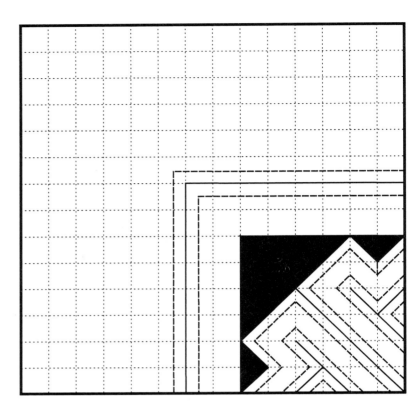

Charted Pattern 28×28

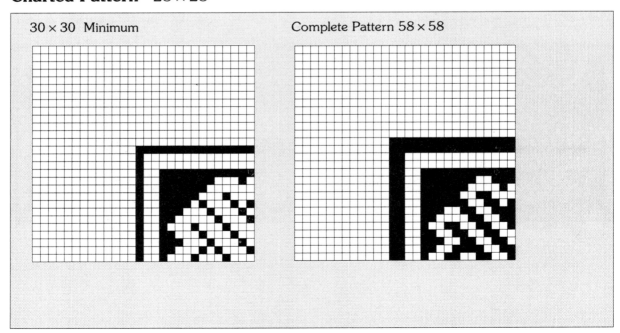

30×30 Minimum

Complete Pattern 58×58

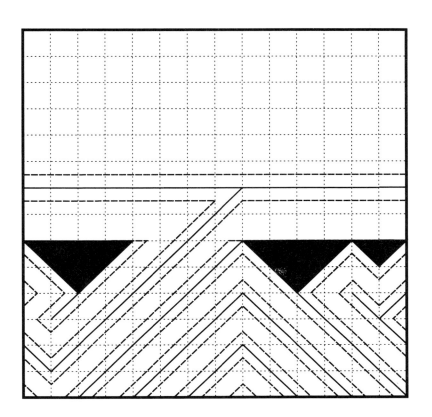

TOP CENTRE

14 × 14

Charted Pattern 28 × 28

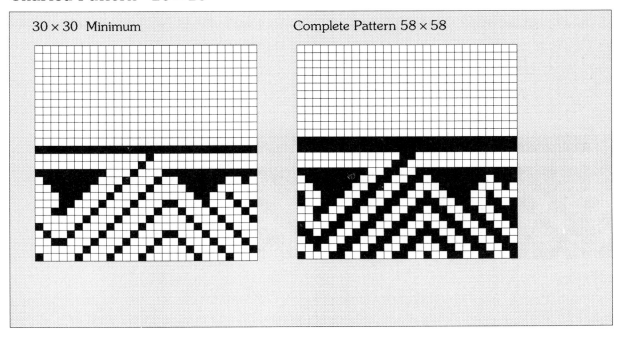

30 × 30 Minimum

Complete Pattern 58 × 58

TOP RIGHT

14 × 14

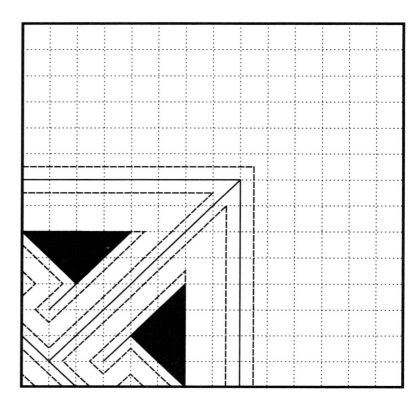

Charted Pattern   28 × 28

30 × 30 Minimum

Complete Pattern 58 × 58

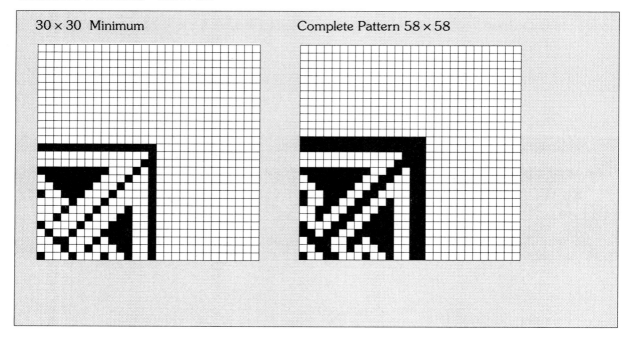

MIDDLE LEFT

14 × 14

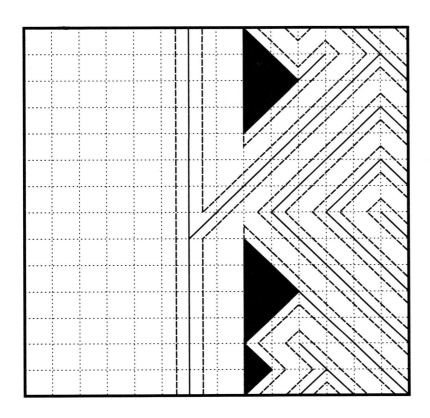

Charted Pattern 28 × 28

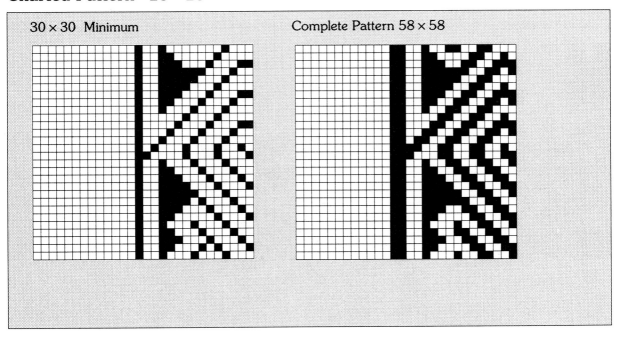

30 × 30 Minimum

Complete Pattern 58 × 58

MIDDLE CENTRE

14 × 14

Charted Pattern   28 × 28

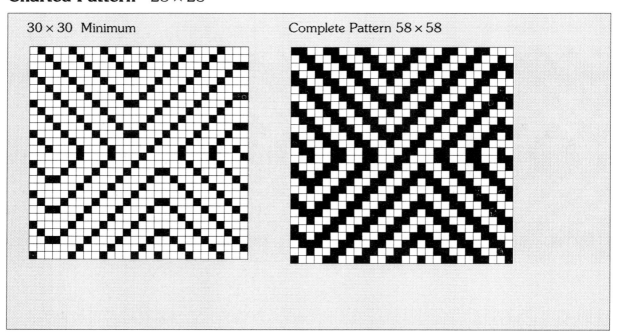

30 × 30 Minimum

Complete Pattern 58 × 58

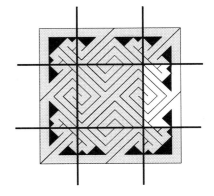

Charted Pattern 28×28

30×30 Minimum

Complete Pattern 58×58

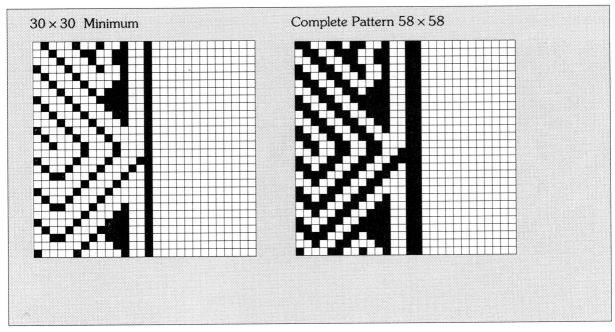

BOTTOM LEFT

14 × 14

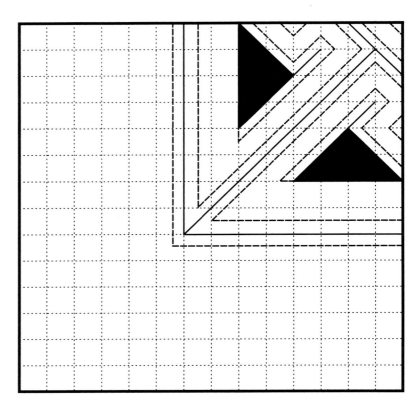

Charted Pattern   28 × 28

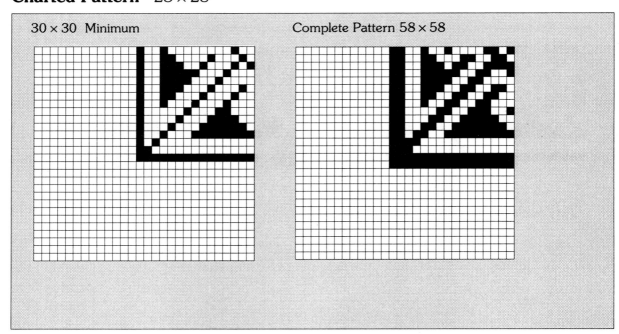

30 × 30 Minimum

Complete Pattern 58 × 58

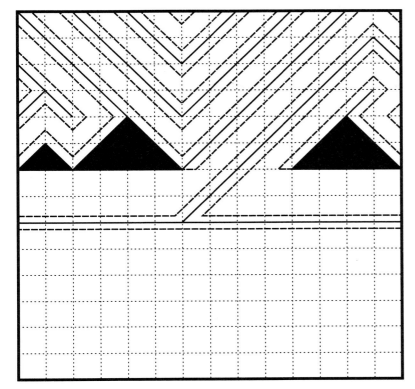

BOTTOM CENTRE

14 × 14

Charted Pattern 28 × 28

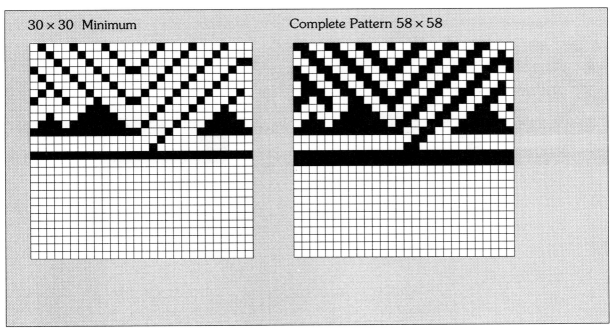

30 × 30 Minimum

Complete Pattern 58 × 58

KEY PATTERN 2244612

BOTTOM RIGHT

14 × 14

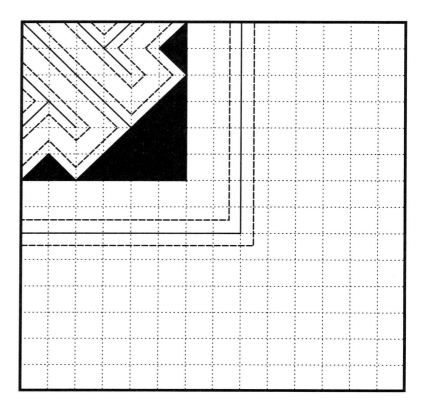

Charted Pattern 28 × 28

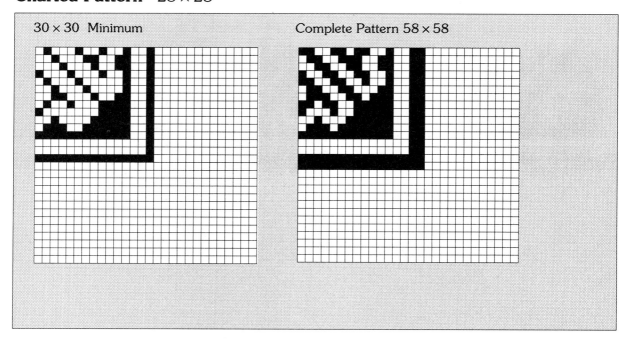

30 × 30 Minimum

Complete Pattern 58 × 58

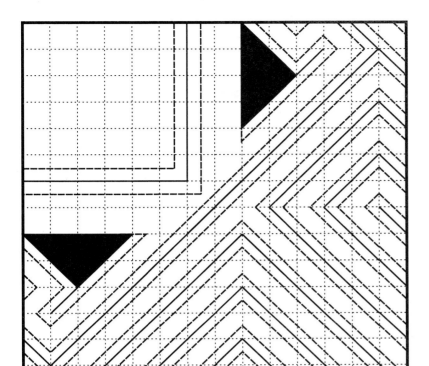

Charted Pattern 28×28

30×30 Minimum

Complete Pattern 58×58

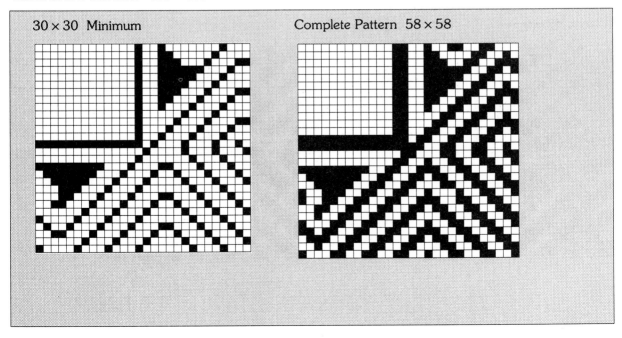

INNER TOP RIGHT

14 × 14

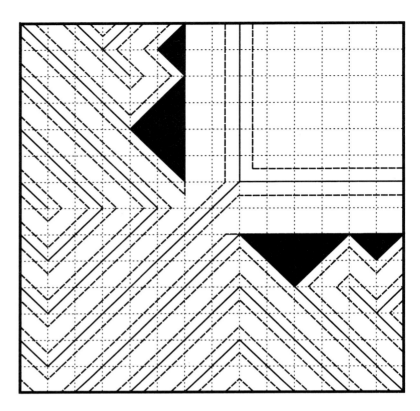

Charted Pattern   28 × 28

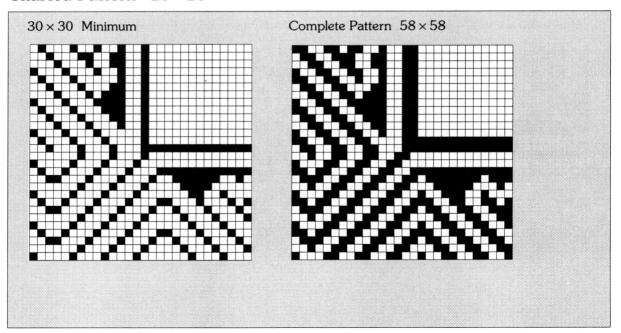

30 × 30 Minimum

Complete Pattern 58 × 58

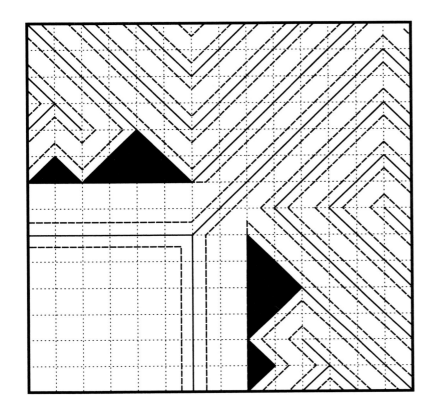

Charted Pattern 28 × 28

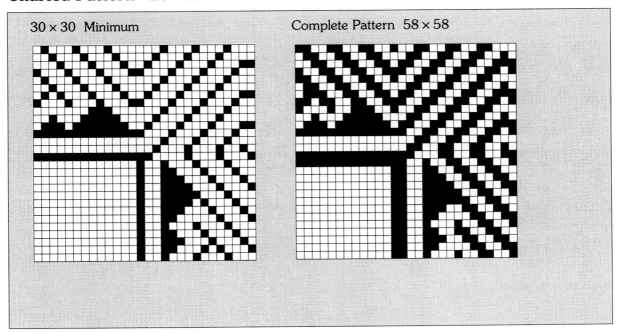

30 × 30 Minimum

Complete Pattern 58 × 58

INNER BOTTOM RIGHT

14 × 14

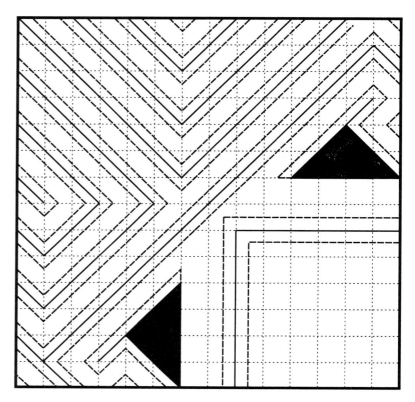

Charted Pattern   28 × 28

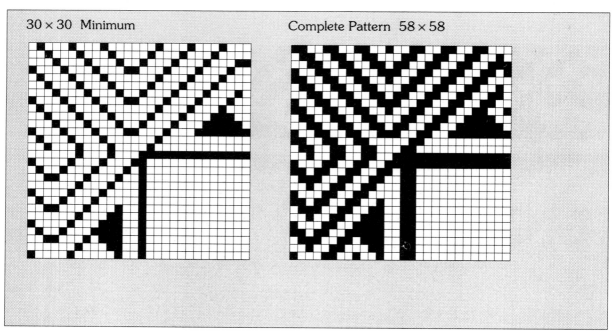

30 × 30 Minimum

Complete Pattern 58 × 58

TOP LEFT

11×11

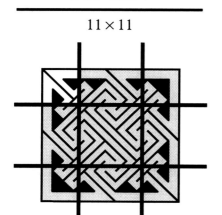

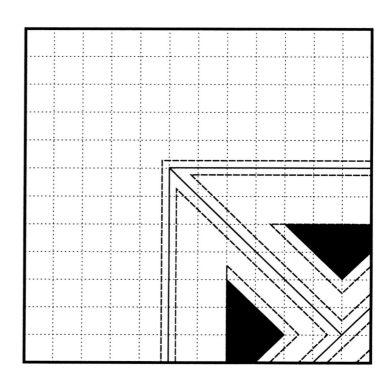

Charted Pattern 22×22

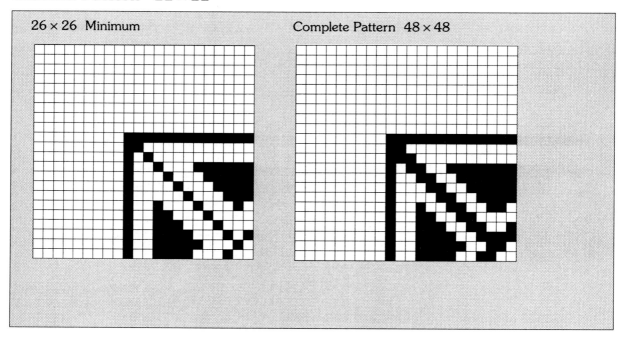

26 × 26 Minimum

Complete Pattern 48 × 48

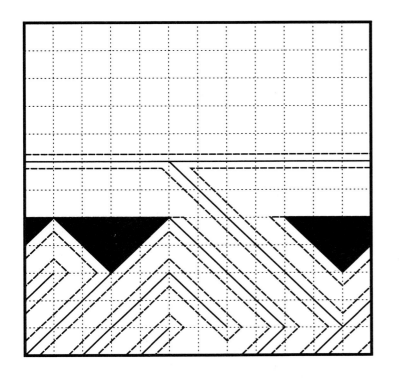

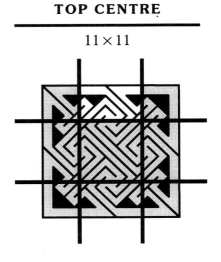

Charted Pattern 22×22

26×26 Minimum

Complete Pattern 48×48

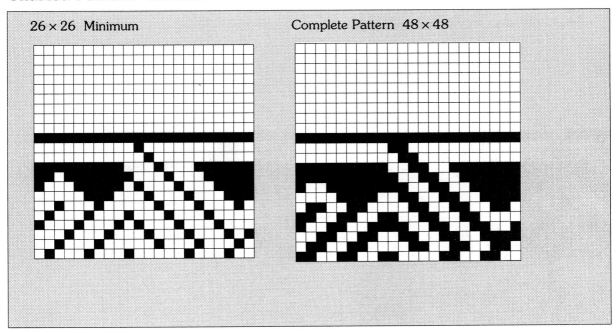

TOP RIGHT

11×11

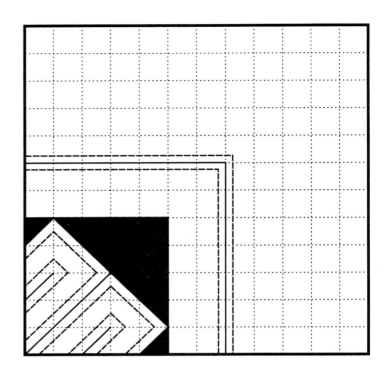

Charted Pattern 22×22

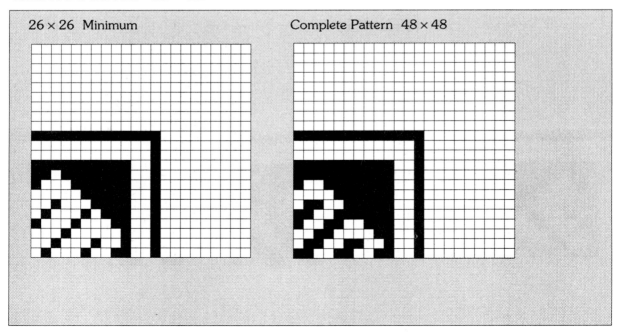

26×26 Minimum

Complete Pattern 48×48

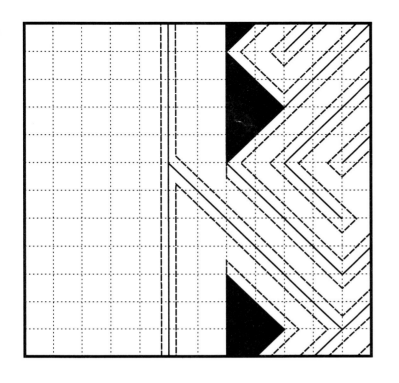

MIDDLE LEFT

11×11

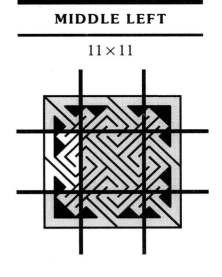

Charted Pattern 22×22

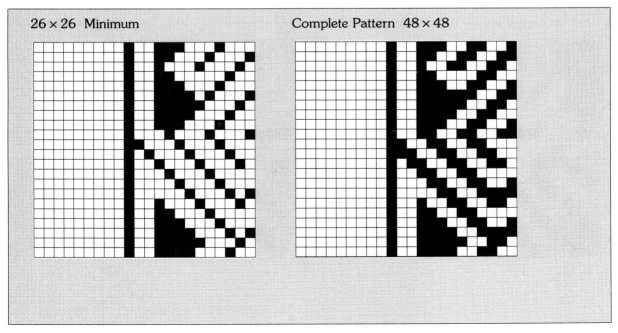

26 × 26 Minimum

Complete Pattern 48 × 48

MIDDLE CENTRE

11×11

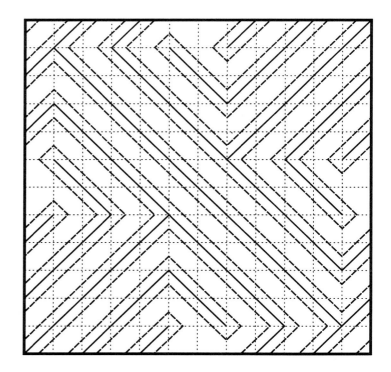

Charted Pattern 22×22

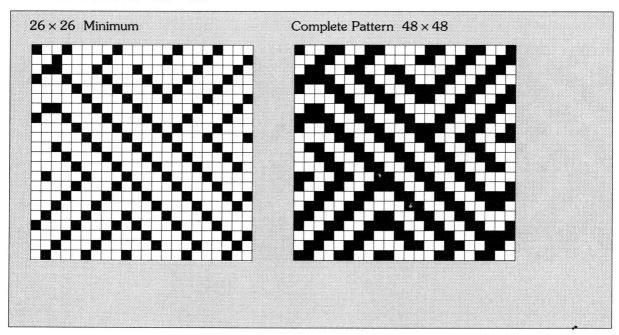

26×26 Minimum

Complete Pattern 48×48

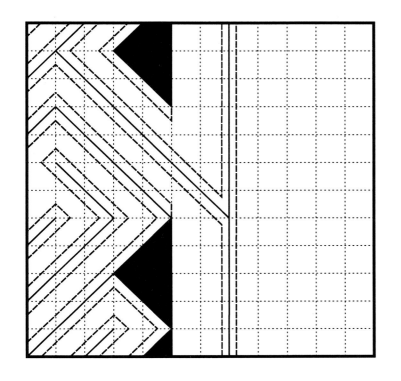

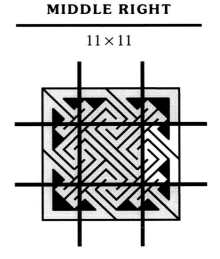

Charted Pattern 22×22

26 × 26 Minimum

Complete Pattern 48 × 48

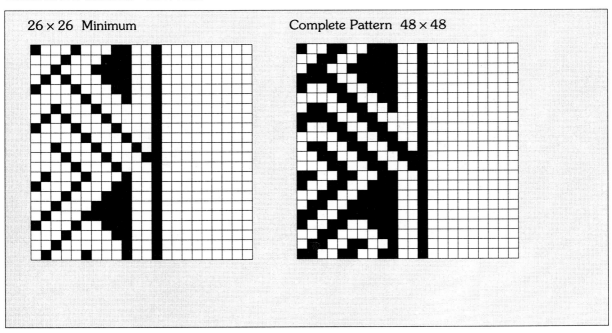

BOTTOM LEFT

11 × 11

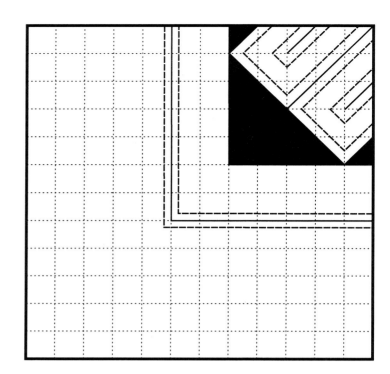

Charted Pattern   22 × 22

26 × 26 Minimum

Complete Pattern 48 × 48

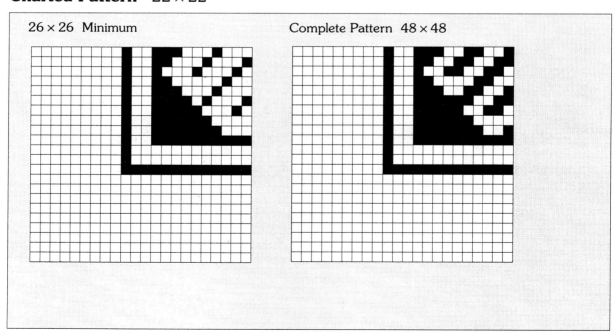

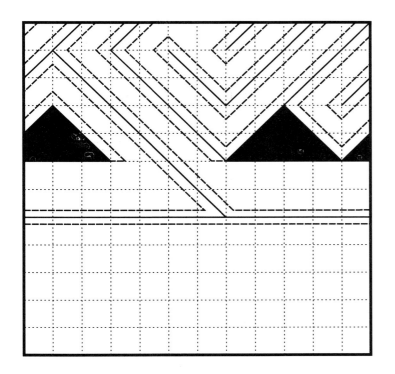

Charted Pattern 22×22

26×26 Minimum

Complete Pattern 48×48

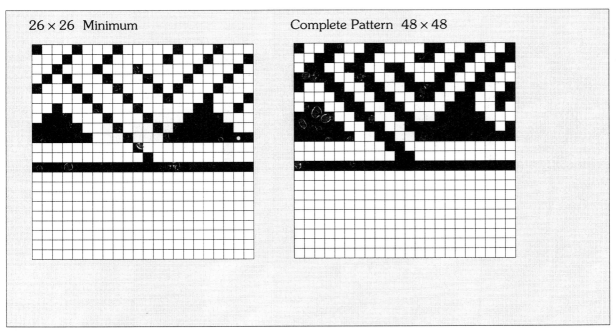

BOTTOM RIGHT

11 × 11

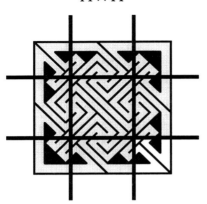

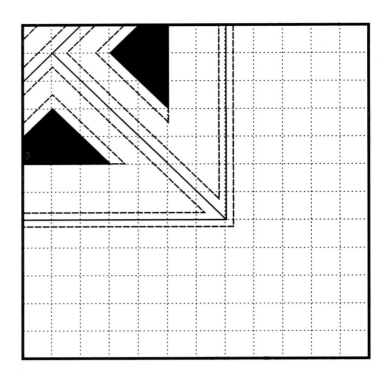

Charted Pattern   22 × 22

26 × 26 Minimum

Complete Pattern 48 × 48

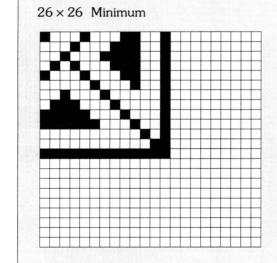

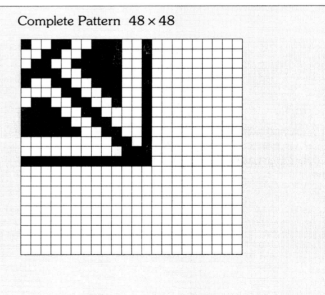

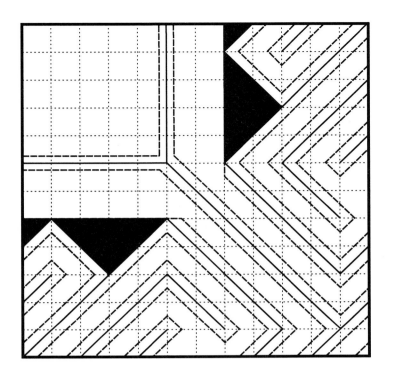

Charted Pattern 22×22

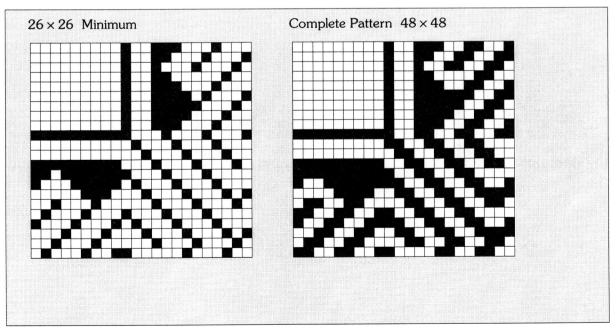

26 × 26 Minimum

Complete Pattern 48 × 48

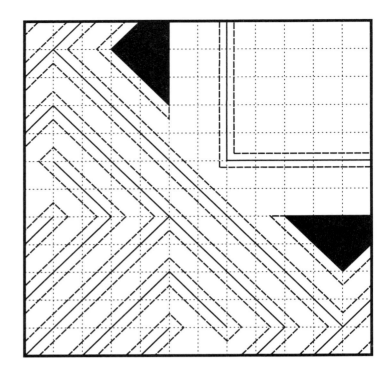

Charted Pattern 22 × 22

26 × 26 Minimum

Complete Pattern 48 × 48

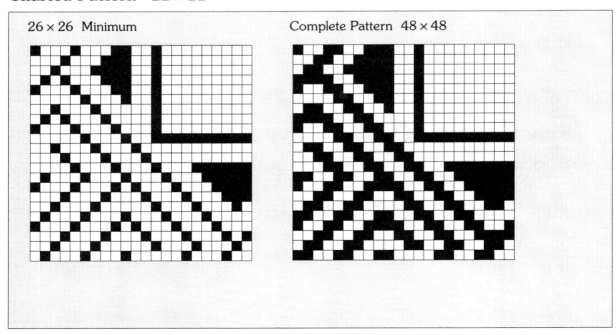

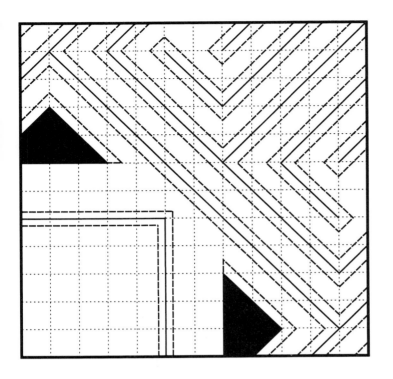

Charted Pattern 22×22

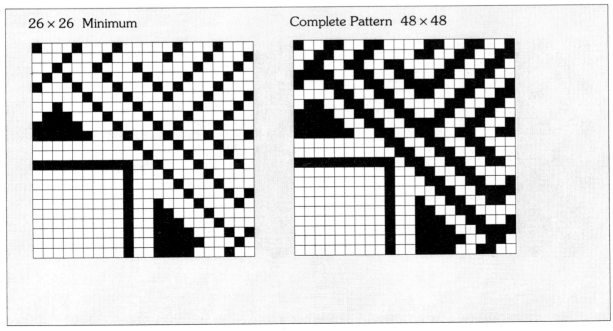

26×26 Minimum

Complete Pattern 48×48

INNER BOTTOM RIGHT

11 × 11

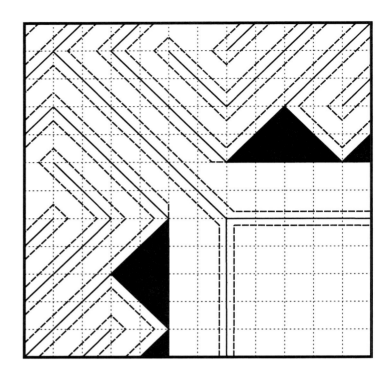

Charted Pattern 22 × 22

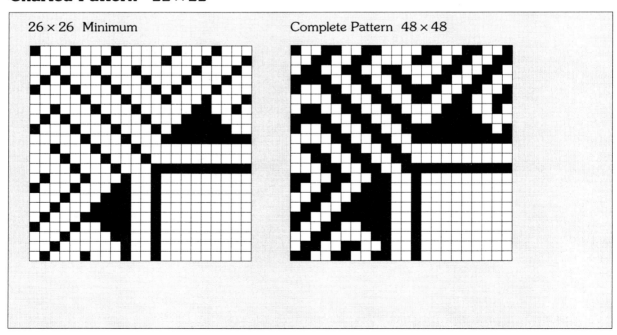

26 × 26 Minimum

Complete Pattern 48 × 48

INDEX